Northwoods Fish Cookery

RON BERG

Northwoods Fish Cookery

University of Minnesota Press
Minneapolis • London

Published by the University of Minnesota Press
111 Third Avenue South, Suite 290
Minneapolis, MN 55401-2520
http://www.upress.umn.edu

Library of Congress Cataloging-in-Publication Data

Berg, Ron, 1942–
    Northwoods fish cookery / Ron Berg.
        p.   cm.
    Includes index.
    ISBN 0-8166-3583-8 (pbk. : acid-free paper)
    1. Cookery (Fish)   2. Cookery—Minnesota.   I. Title.
    TX747 .B387 2000
    641.6′92—dc21   99-050532

Printed in the United States of America on acid-free paper

The University of Minnesota is an equal-opportunity educator and employer.

11 10 09 08 07 06 05 04 03 02 01 00   10 9 8 7 6 5 4 3 2 1

To the memory of my friend Bob Westgard (1940–1999)

Contents

Chapter 2. Camp and Shore Cookery

Chapter 3. Fishing Camp and Cabin Recipes

Chapter 4. Appetizers, Soups, and First Courses

Chapter 5. Elegant Entrées

Chapter 6. Favorite Recipes from Minnesota Restaurants and Resorts

Angry Trout Cafe, Grand Marais

Coho Cafe, Tofte

Chapter 7. The Smoker

Chapter 8. Accompaniments

Chapter 9. Stuffings, Breadings, and Seasonings

Chapter 10. Sauces for Fish

Acknowledgments

I want to thank my editor, Todd Orjala, for his encouragement and assistance in getting this project off the ground and on its way. I am deeply indebted to Gene Zelek, who freely provided me with his valuable professional advice. Gene, I owe you many, many personally guided fishing trips. Thank you also to chefs Judy Barsness, Tracy Jacobson, Kieran Moore, Bob Bennett, and Travis Johnson, and to George Wilkes, owner of the Angry Trout Cafe, and Craig and Brad Schutte, owners of the 510 Restaurant, for taking the time to contribute recipes to this book. Finally, I would be remiss if I didn't thank Keli Meyer for her loving support and encouragement in the writing of this book.

Ron Berg
1 June 1999
Seagull Lake

Introduction

Ever since I can remember I have loved to cook. Over the seventeen summers I worked as a fishing guide, this proved to be a definite asset. If I couldn't be the best fisherman on the lake, I was determined to be the best cook. Cooking fish over an open fire became my specialty.

In 1991 I left a twenty-four-year teaching career to become head chef at Gunflint Lodge. Over the years that I had worked as a fishing guide and then as a chef in the northwoods of Minnesota, I learned much about the lakes I fished, how to keep freshly caught fish in tip-top eating condition, and, best of all, how to cook and eat them in interesting and delicious ways. This book is, in essence, a compilation of all that I have learned along the way.

In Minnesota where I live, people love to fish. According to the Minnesota Department of Natural Resources, in the Land of 10,000 Lakes there are 3,800,000 acres of fishable water on 6,000 lakes, plus 15,000 miles of fishable streams, which include 1,900 miles of trout streams. Minnesota has, in fact, a total of 2.3 million anglers and ranks first nationally in the sales of fishing licenses per capita. In 1995, for example, 1,444,770 fishing licenses were sold in the state and 35 million pounds of sport fish were harvested. The fish that are caught the most in the state are panfish, followed by wall-eye (the state fish) and northern pike.

If you are new to fishing, I will show you how to take care of the fish you catch and how to keep them fresh tasting for future eating. Basic cooking methods for fish are explained with simple recipes. And if you are an old hand at fishing or just looking for new and exciting ways to cook fish, you will find many recipes, ranging from the simple to the elegant.

If you are cooking in a fishing camp for your buddies or staying at your cabin "up north," you will find a number of quick and easy recipes with simple ingredients that are sure to keep you off dishwashing duty. In addition, you'll learn how to cook fish over a campfire in a remote camp and how to prepare an authentic guide's shore lunch.

Best of all, even if you don't fish you can enjoy the recipes in this book. Fresh and frozen walleye, rainbow trout, salmon, whitefish, northern pike, lake trout, and catfish are among the many kinds of game fish that can be purchased in fish markets and many supermarkets.

How This Book Is Arranged

In chapter 1, "The Basics," you will find information on the variety of game fish found in Minnesota waters, the best ways to care for and store fish, and the basic cooking methods and recipes for preparing your catch.

Chapter 2, "Camp and Shore Cookery," gives instructions and recipes for cooking fish over a campfire, including directions for preparing a shore lunch.

Chapter 3, "Fishing Camp and Cabin Recipes," features quick and easy recipes to prepare while staying in a resort or at your cabin "up north."

Chapter 4, "Appetizers, Soups, and First Courses," presents interesting ways to prepare fish for a first course or for enjoying by themselves as a light meal.

Chapter 5, "Elegant Entrées," contains a selection of recipes for delicious entrées that vary from simple preparations to recipes requiring several steps.

Chapter 6, "Favorite Recipes from Minnesota Restaurants and Resorts," showcases recipes from a few of Minnesota's premier restaurants and resorts.

Chapter 7, "The Smoker," shows you how to smoke fish and use them in recipes, as well as how to prepare a variety of smoked vegetables.

The last three chapters—chapter 8, "Accompaniments," chapter 9, "Stuffings, Breadings, and Seasonings," and chapter 10, "Sauces for Fish"—provide numerous recipes to enhance and complement your fish dishes.

And finally, as you try recipes from this book, keep in mind this sage advice from Chef Jonathan Locke, who said it best: "Any recipe is a snare and a delusion. Recipes . . . are simply one cook's approximation of ingredients, amounts, and methods which achieve pleasing results. But ingredients don't combine by themselves, they need guidance. Rely on your palate, if you follow a recipe scrupulously and, when you taste it, something is missing, then it is, and it's your ball game. Think of recipes as guideposts, not gospel."

Chapter 1

The Basics

When I first began guiding fishermen back in 1975, it didn't take me long to figure out that I still had a lot to learn. Like most fishermen I knew then, I put the fish I caught on a stringer. As I moved from spot to spot, the fish we had caught would be hauled in and out of the boat. Back and forth they would go, from the warm surface water to lying in the sun at the bottom of the boat. Needless to say, it wouldn't be long before the entire day's catch was floating belly up.

Back in camp at the cleaning table, the consequences of this mistreatment were evident. The fish on the stringer were stiff and nearly white. The gills were barely pink and the once-firm flesh was so soft that my fingers would sink right through it when I held the fillet to remove the rib bones. I knew there had to be a better way.

Fish are highly perishable and proper care begins as soon as the hook is removed. The information in this chapter will show you how to keep your freshly caught fish tasting fresh right up until it is cooked. And speaking of cooking, "Basic Fish Cookery at a Glance" (p. 10) is the place to begin if you have questions about how to cook your fish or if you are looking for new cooking methods to try. Concise and comprehensive, this section covers the basic cooking methods for fish alphabetically.

Minnesota's Game Fish

Minnesota's best-known game fish include walleye, sauger, northern pike, muskellunge, lake trout, smallmouth and largemouth bass, stream trout, splake (a cross between a speckled or brook trout and a lake trout) and panfish—crappies, sunfish, and yellow perch. Whitefish, while technically not a game fish, are included here because they have great flavor and texture and are a good substitute for walleye. They are also excellent when smoked. Also fished in Minnesota to a lesser degree (primarily in the southern tier of the state) are bullheads and catfish, which are excellent eating fish.

Walleye

(Also known as marble eyes, pike-perch, and yellow pike)

Minnesota's premier game fish (and the official state fish) is the walleye, a fish known not so much for its fighting ability as for its eatability. It is a strong but decidedly unspectacular fighter. Often called a walleye pike, the walleye is, in fact, a member of the perch family, not the pike family.

The walleye opener in May is a nearly sacred day for many avid fishermen. Unfortunately, Mother's Day is often celebrated on the Sunday of that same weekend. Let's face it, choosing between motherhood and fishing is difficult. A surprising number of men send a card and flowers and promise themselves to think of their mothers and/or wives in between bites.

Walleyes are not well known in most states. Catfish and whitefish fillets are available nationwide and are an excellent substitute for walleye in any of the recipes in this book. Fresh and frozen walleye is available in many supermarkets. Walleye is a favorite offering in Minnesota restaurants.

Sauger

Not as widespread as walleye, the sauger resembles the walleye in appearance and habits. They are smaller than walleye and usually do not exceed 3 pounds. They are excellent eating.

Northern Pike

(Also known as jackfish, northerns, hammerhandles [little northerns], and, by disparagers, slimers)

Northern pike will grow to 30 to 40 pounds or more. Their most infamous features are the Y-bones, which run down the upper third of the fillet, and their annoying habit of relieving walleye fishermen of their terminal tackle. The bones are most troublesome in small northerns, thus the best eating size runs from 3 to 5 pounds. The bigger the fish, the bigger the bones and the easier to detect and remove them. A skillful filleter can remove the Y-bones with ease, but most erstwhile attempts produce a dreadful mess of mangled fish flesh. Northern pike are often pickled because the pickling process so softens the bones that they disappear entirely. I urge you not to let disparaging remarks turn you against northern pike. They are eminently delicious.

In fact, the French consider them gourmet fare. In the Anjou and Nantes regions of France, a whole northern pike is poached in a court bouillon (p. 217), a vegetable broth made with water and a little vinegar or lemon juice, then served with an exquisitely delicate butter sauce, a Beurre Nantais (p. 236), which is similar to a beurre blanc.

Filleting Northern Pike without Y-Bones

One summer I had the pleasure of working with a young fishing guide from Whitefish Lake, Ontario, who taught me an easy way to eliminate the Y-bones when filleting a northern pike. He ended up with five pieces, but since two of them were fairly small and consisted primarily of just belly meat, I have modified his method. Nothing will be wasted if you make a stock from the pike, minus the guts, gills, and skin (see "Stocks," p. 216). Any meat remaining on the carcass can be removed after making the stock and used in a fish loaf, soup, or chowder.

To begin, lay the northern pike on its belly (no need to gut it beforehand). With a sharp fillet knife, cut down to the backbone directly behind the head. Now lay the knife flat to the backbone and cut down to a point directly in front of the dorsal fin. Remove the knife and cut straight down to the spine in front of the fin to free the fillet.

Next lay the fish on its side and cut down to the spine starting where the first fillet left off and lay the knife flat to the spine to remove the side by cutting down to the tail and removing the fillet. Repeat with the other side.

You have now removed most of the meat from the pike and have three large boneless fillets. I also prefer to remove the thin strip of cartilage that runs down the center of the top fillet. Use your knife to cut along both sides of this down to the skin to remove it. You will end up with two long back strip fillets, which we could refer to as northern pike tenderloins.

Next, remove the skin from the fillet pieces by laying them skin side down and running your fillet knife between the flesh and the skin. A pliers is handy for holding the skin while removing the fillet.

Muskellunge

(Also known as muskie)

Similar to northern pike in appearance, muskies have been introduced to more than 50 lakes in Minnesota. They can be a difficult fish to catch, which makes them all the more desirable. In Minnesota, lakes with muskie populations have special regulations with strict size limits. Muskies can be used in any recipe calling for northern pike. The hybrid tiger muskie is a cross between a northern pike and a muskellunge.

Smallmouth Bass and Largemouth Bass

Both the smallmouth (also known as bronzeback) and the large-mouth bass are members of the sunfish family. In a very general sense, smallmouth bass inhabit the northern part of the state, while the warmer water–loving largemouth bass inhabit the weedier warmer lakes of the southern half. Both are tremendous fighters. It has been said that, pound for pound, no fish can match the fight of a smallmouth bass. Smallmouth bass, for the most part, are excellent eating. The largemouth bass, like the crappie, are best eaten during early summer before the water gets too warm.

Lake Trout
(Also known as lakers)

Often referred to by the misnomer of "landlocked salmon," the lake trout is not related to the salmon family, but is a true trout. The flesh of the lake trout runs from nearly white to a deep orange color. Lake trout inhabit the cold, clear, deep lakes in northern Minnesota and Canada. They can grow as large as 40 to 60 pounds. Lake trout require pristine water conditions and are among the first fish affected by pollution of any sort. Lake trout do not freeze well and are best eaten fresh or within a month of freezing.

Fish Eating Advisories

Unfortunately many of our fishing waters have now become polluted enough for state health authorities to issue eating advisories. These advisories vary from lake to lake and species to species, and even on the size of the fish. For up-to-date information, contact your state's department of health.

For fish advisories in Minnesota contact:

Minnesota Department of Health
717 Delaware Street Southeast
Minneapolis, MN 55440-9441
(651) 676-5000
www.health.state.mn.us/

Stream Trout and Splake

Minnesota's stream trout include brook trout (also known as speckled trout), rainbow trout or steelhead, brown trout, and the hybrid splake, a cross between a speckled (brook) trout and a lake trout.

Brook trout are Minnesota's only native trout. Those that inhabit Lake Superior and return to streams to spawn are called "coasters." Rainbow trout living in Lake Superior that return to spawn in streams are known as "steelhead."

Stream trout are considered to be one of the finest eating fish. Although stream trout in lakes can reach 10 pounds or more, most stream trout seldom run more than a pound or two. Smaller stream trout are usually prepared whole, and a single fish would constitute an individual serving. A neat trick is to completely debone the trout (see "Simple Surgery: Removing Bones from Trout" on p. 123), fill it with a savory stuffing, and bake it. Larger trout may also be stuffed or filleted to be grilled, broiled, seared, or panfried. As with all trout, there is no need to scale them, because their scales are so small and soft.

Panfish

The most commonly caught panfish are sunfish (bluegills and pumpkinseed being the most common species), crappies, and yellow perch.

Would kids ever get interested in fishing if panfish didn't exist? These pint-sized, easy-to-catch fish are delicious eating. I have fond memories of fish fries as a youngster. Huge platters of panfried sunnies or crappies that had been scaled, gutted, deheaded, and then fried to a crisp golden brown were served on quiet summer evenings after a day at the lake. The crisp tails were especially esteemed and everyone seemed to have their own technique for separating the meat from the bones. Large panfish can be filleted before or after scaling and the rib bones removed, resulting in boneless morsels that are wonderful when breaded or battered and deep-fried.

Whitefish

(Also known as lake whitefish)

Whitefish inhabit a variety of waters and run from 1 to 6 pounds. They are a fairly oily fish. On many northern Minnesota lakes, whitefish provide fast fishing action in late August and September, when they move in great numbers onto deepwater reefs to spawn. They are most often available for purchase as smoked whole fish, but fresh or frozen fillets can often be found. Lake Superior whitefish (and lake trout) are oilier than those fish caught on inland lakes.

Catfish

(Also known as mudcat or yellow cat)

Common to the large slow rivers of southern Minnesota, the two species of catfish caught in Minnesota waters are the flathead catfish, which can reach 100 pounds or more, and the channel catfish, which usually runs from 1 to 4 pounds but can reach upward of 20 pounds. Catfish are excellent eating and farm-raised catfish are readily available commercially.

Bullheads

Bullheads are common in slow running creeks and lakes too oxygen-poor to support more popular game fish. Yellow, black, and brown species of bullhead are all found in Minnesota waters. Compared to other game fish, bullheads have smooth, tough, leathery skin and a reputation for "stinging" unwary anglers with sharp bones near the gills. They are, however, excellent table fare with a delicious meaty flavor.

For more detailed information on Minnesota game fish, visit the Minnesota Department of Natural Resources (DNR) Web site at http://www.dnr.state.mn.us/fish_and_wildlife/fish/

Taking Care of Your Catch

Proper Care of Freshly Caught Fish

There are only two ways to keep the fish you catch impeccably fresh: by keeping them alive or by keeping them on ice. Stringers and live wells are of limited value in keeping fish alive, especially when the surface water is warm. The fish are soon floating belly up and your fine meal is well on its way to being ruined. It is far better to kill a fish as soon as it is removed from the hook with a blow to the head and then put it into a cooler packed with ice, preferably crushed or small cubes. Think of 32°F as a set point; keeping fish close to that temperature slows down the inevitable process of deterioration until the fish are cleaned and eaten or frozen.

Storage Time of Cleaned Fish for Freshest Flavor

After cleaning, the fish (whole or broken down into fillets or steaks) may be wrapped loosely and stored under refrigeration (30° to 34°F) for 3 to 4 days. By icing the fish, the preferred storage time under refrigeration (32°F) increases to 5 or 6 days. The fish to be iced should be placed in a self-draining container, such as a colander set over a bowl. When adding ice, be careful not to bruise the fish with the ice.

Fresh fish may be stored for considerably longer at the temperatures and conditions above without spoiling, but flavor will deteriorate over time, and freezing becomes the best option after the storage periods listed above.

Note that these are optimum conditions and that most home refrigerators usually run at warmer (38° to 40°F) temperatures. In that case the ice should be checked and replaced at frequent intervals. Non-iced fish stored at these temperatures should be eaten or frozen within a few days for best flavor; iced fish should be consumed or frozen after 3 to 4 days.

The Wire-Snap Stringer Trophy Tragedy

Few guides I know have ever had much use for stringers of any design because they are probably the worst way ever invented to take care of freshly caught fish. There are other reasons as well. Once a client of mine insisted on putting a ten-pound-plus walleye he had just caught on a wire-snap stringer. He didn't want his walleye of a lifetime scrunched into a cooler or put on one of those "flimsy" nylon stringers, he said. I suspected another reason and soon enough it became evident. As another boat trolled by, he proudly pulled his recent catch out of the water by the stringer and held it up so the fishermen in the other boat could properly admire it. The weight of the fish pulled the snap open and suddenly the trophy fish he had dreamed of catching for years splashed back into the water and disappeared into the depths.

Freezing Fish for Single Servings

Here are three convenient ways to freeze your summer catch in individual portions. Before transporting fish, check your state's regulations. For best eating, use frozen fish within 3 months (lake trout within 1 month).

Film-and-Foil Method

Wrap each fillet tightly in a double layer of plastic wrap. Lay them flat on a cookie sheet. Place in freezer. When frozen, wrap each fillet with aluminum foil. Place the wrapped fillets in plastic freezer bags. Squeeze out as much air as possible and twist the top of the bag until it is tight and forms a loop. Twist a wire twist-tie around this loop. Place this bag inside another freezer bag and repeat this process with the second bag. This makes a fairly effective airtight seal.

Water-Glazing Method

Glazing with water provides airtight protection against freezer burn. Commercially frozen fish are often water glazed.

Lay the fillets on a cookie sheet, cover with plastic film, and freeze. When frozen, dip each fillet several times in ice water or use a spray bottle to coat the fillet with cold water on both sides and return to freezer. Repeat the process 3 to 4 times until the fillets are well glazed with ice. Place glazed fillets in freezer bags and twist and seal as described above.

Ready-to-Cook Method

Frozen breaded fish are great to have on hand. No thawing is necessary before using; simply deep-fry the fish until golden brown. The breading also forms a formidable barrier against freezer burn.

Bread whole fish fillets (not over ⅜ inch thick for proper deep-frying), chunks, or finger-sized strips using the Three-Step Breading recipe described on page 210. Lay individually on a cookie sheet. Cover with plastic film or foil and place in freezer. When frozen, remove and place in freezer bags. Squeeze out as much air as possible. Twist and seal in double plastic bags as described in "Film-and-Foil Method" on page 9. Do not thaw fish before using. To cook, simply deep-fry at 360°F.

Bread and freeze finger-sized strips of fish and eat them like the shrimp they resemble with lemon wedges and tartar or cocktail sauce. These are wonderful served with cocktails or as an appetizer.

Freezing in Quantity

Use the following freezing techniques when you want to package and freeze fish for a fish fry or in family-sized portions.

Plastic Bag/Freezer Wrap Method

Use a plastic bag to hold the number of fish fillets you want to freeze. Extract as much air as possible and seal the bag tightly with a wire twist-tie. Now twist and seal as described in "Film-and-Foil Method" on page 9, using one bag rather than two. Wrap in a double layer of freezer wrap, then seal and label. An easy way to get most of the air out of a bag is to submerge the bag containing the fish in a large container of cold water. The water will force the air out of the bag.

Freezing-in-Water Method

I am not a fan of freezing fish in water because the delicate flavor can be soaked out. However, this method has many advocates and does provide a good way to avoid freezer burn.

Use freezer-weight zipper-top plastic bags (1- or 2-quart size). Place fish in the bags, cover with cold water, fold the top to force out most of the air, then seal and freeze.

Well-washed half-gallon paperboard milk cartons can also be used. Open the top completely and fill about ½ to ¾ full with fish fillets or prepared panfish. Cover the fish completely with cold water and fold down the top to seal. Use masking tape to hold the top of the carton down. When you use either method, be sure to leave a little headroom to allow for expansion of the ice. Place upright in the freezer.

Basic Fish Cookery at a Glance

This is where to begin if you have questions about cooking fish or are looking for a basic recipe. Cooking methods are listed alphabetically.

Baking

This method works well with all fish. This is very similar to roasting, but the fish are often cooked at a lower temperature with or without any added liquid.

Basic Baked Fish Fillets

Preheat oven to 375°F. Butter a shallow-sided bake-and-serve dish and lay fillets skin side down in a slightly overlapping layer. Brush the tops of the fillets with a lemon butter mixture (about 1 teaspoon freshly squeezed lemon juice, or to taste, to every 4 tablespoons of butter). Season lightly with salt and freshly ground black pepper and sprinkle with paprika. Bake in preheated oven for 10 to 20 minutes or until fish is a little underdone. Check frequently to avoid overcooking. Remember the fish will continue to cook after you remove it from the oven.

Garlic-Parmesan Baked Fish Fillets

Preheat oven to 375°F. Combine 4 tablespoons of melted butter with 1 large clove of garlic, minced, and 1 teaspoon of fresh lemon juice, or to taste. Brush a shallow-sided bake-and-serve dish with some of the garlic-lemon butter and lay the fillets skin side down in a slightly overlapping layer. Brush the tops of the fish with additional garlic-lemon butter and season lightly with salt and freshly ground black pepper. Sprinkle with freshly grated Parmesan cheese to taste. Bake in preheated oven for 10 to 20 minutes or until fish is a little underdone.

Boiling

In parts of northern Wisconsin, fish boils are a tradition. Chef Glen D'Amour of the Kamloops Restaurant, located at Superior Shores Resort in Two Harbors, has reintroduced that tradition to Minnesota's scenic North Shore. Glen hosts weekly fish boils during the summer months.

The most commonly used fish are whitefish and lake trout. Here's how it is done. A large pot of fairly heavily salted water is hung or set over a roaring wood fire and brought to a boil. A basket of potatoes and onions is lowered into the water. When the potatoes and onions are cooked, another basket containing the fish is lowered into the pot on top of the first basket. For the grand finale, kerosene is thrown on the fire, causing it to flare up. This blast of heat causes the pot to boil over, quickly cooking the fish and dousing the fire at the same time. The fish, potatoes, and onions are served with lots of melted butter, coleslaw, and bread.

Broiling

This method works well with all fish fillets, especially thinner ones. With this method, fish are broiled beneath the broiler of your stove. Because most game fish fillets are thin, the fillets do not usually need to be turned during the broiling process. Depending on thickness, fish should be broiled 4 to 6 inches from the heat. Note that broiled fish do not brown on top because of their moisture content.

For a basic recipe, see Walleye Broiled in White Wine on page 66.

Canning

You will need a pressure cooker if you want to can fish. This is especially good with northern pike, salmon, lake trout, and smoked fish, but can be used successfully with any type of fish. Don't worry about the bones; like pickling, the canning process softens the bones.

Use the home-canned fish in place of commercially canned tuna or salmon to prepare tasty casseroles, pasta dishes, fish loaves or cakes, sandwich spreads, or quiches—in fact, in just about any recipe that calls for canned fish.

Prepare pint jars for canning by washing and rinsing them, then microwaving the wet jars for 3 minutes. Sterilize the lids by covering them with water and bringing to a boil. Turn off the heat and let the lids sit for several minutes. Drain and use the lids while still warm. IMPORTANT: *Do not attempt to can fish in jars larger than one pint in order for proper processing to take place.*

Understanding the ingredients gives you the opportunity to make changes based on your personal taste. The vinegar raises the acidity of the canned fish and helps protect against unwanted bacterial growth. I have seen recipes for canned fish that do not call for vinegar, but for safety's sake, I would include it. It gives the fish a pleasant piquant flavor. The salt provides flavor and may be decreased to ½ teaspoon per jar if a lower sodium product is desired. The oil is necessary only if the fish are lean and may be reduced to 1 tablespoon or omitted if a lower fat product is desired. The tomato sauce gives white fish, such as northern pike, the appearance of canned salmon. When using home-canned fish, discard *without tasting* any jars that do not seem to be tightly sealed. Lids now have safety buttons that enable you to see at a glance if the seal is good.

Canned Fish

Cut skinless fish into 1-inch chunks and pack into sterilized pint jars, leaving ½ inch headspace. Each pint will hold about 1½ cups (about 1 pound) of cut-up fish. To each jar add:

> 1 tablespoon white vinegar
> 1 teaspoon kosher or canning salt
> 3 tablespoons vegetable oil (omit if canning oily fish, such as salmon)
> 3 tablespoons canned tomato sauce (omit if canning salmon)

Wipe the rims of the jars very thoroughly with a damp paper towel and seal by placing the lid and band on the jar. Tighten the bands according to the manufacturer's instructions. Place the jars in the pressure cooker and add water as manufacturer recommends. Process at 10 pounds pressure for 90 minutes, and allow pressure to reduce naturally. Remove jars with tongs, place on a towel in an area free from drafts, and let sit undisturbed for 12 hours. Remove bands and check the seals according to the manufacturer's recommendations. Any jars not properly sealed should be promptly refrigerated and eaten within two days. Canned fish, stored in a cool place, will keep for about one year.

Crusting

Crusting can be used with all fish. To make a very basic crusted fish, top fillets with crumbs, drizzle with butter, and roast in a hot oven. The process lends itself to endless variations. Here is a simple recipe that is wonderful with freshly caught fish. Additional recipes for crusted fish can be found in chapter 5, "Elegant Entrées."

Fresh Herb-Crusted Fish Fillets

Preheat oven to 450°F. A lower oven temperature, from 375°F to 400°F should be used for fish fillets over ½ inch thick. The goal is for the fish to complete cooking at the same time the crust becomes golden brown.

Stir about 2 to 3 tablespoons of mixed fresh herbs, such as basil, Italian parsley, and chives (also consider dill, chervil, and tarragon), into each cup of fresh white bread crumbs. Lay fillets on a shallow-sided sheet pan or pie tin that has been sprayed with nonstick cooking spray. Brush each fillet with melted butter and season with salt and freshly ground black pepper. Top each fillet with a liberal layer of the bread-crumb mixture. Drizzle melted butter over the bread crumbs. Bake in preheated oven until fish are barely done.

En Papillote (In Parchment)

This French term refers to fish (or other foods) cooked in an oiled parchment packet. The food is often served right in the parchment package and is best opened at the moment it is being served to allow the diner to savor the steamy aromas as the parchment is cut open. Foil may be substituted for the parchment. See Foil-Baked Fish Fillets, page 64, for numerous ways to use this easy and unique cooking method. This is an elegant and delicious way to prepare any game fish.

Fish en Papillote

> 6 rectangular sheets of parchment paper
> 3 tablespoons butter
> 1 clove garlic, finely chopped
> 1 cup leeks, white part only, julienned
> 1 cup celery, julienned
> 1 cup carrots, julienned
> 6 boneless, skinless fish fillets (6 to 7 ounces each)
> Salt and freshly ground black pepper to taste
> 6 tablespoons dry white wine
> 6 fresh thyme sprigs

Preheat oven to 425°F. Fold each sheet of parchment in half and cut into a heart shape large enough to encase a portion of fish when folded in half.

In a medium sauté pan, heat the butter over medium-low heat, add the garlic, leeks, celery, and carrots, and season with salt and pepper to taste. Toss and stir the vegetables to coat them with butter. Cover pan and let vegetables sweat for about 5 minutes, or until the vegetables are almost soft. Set aside to cool for 5 minutes.

Spray the parchment hearts lightly with nonstick cooking spray. Season each side of the fillets lightly with salt and pepper. Place 1 fillet on each parchment heart and spoon one-sixth of the sautéed mixture over each fish, drizzle 1 tablespoon of wine over each fillet, and top with a sprig of thyme. Fold the parchment over and seal the edges by crimping them. Place parchment packages on a large sheet pan (or two if necessary) and bake in preheated oven for 10 to 12 minutes. If the parchment was well sealed, the packages may puff. Remove from oven and use a spatula to place a parchment package on each heated serving plate. Use a scissors or sharp knife to cut a large X in the top of the parchment. Serves 6.

Deep-Frying

The best fish for deep-frying are lean white fish, such as walleye, bass, northern pike, catfish, and panfish. To my mind, the best way to fry fish is over an open fire, preferably on the shore of one of Minnesota's sparkling blue lakes with the smell of wood smoke and pine in the air. To do the job in your own kitchen, an electric deep fryer appliance is perhaps the easiest way to go. Just add the oil, set the temperature, bread or batter the fish, and fry. A 4-inch deep cast-iron pan, often called a "chicken fryer," works well if you don't own an electric fryer.

I prefer a temperature of 360°F for deep-frying. If you are using a pan on the stove top, clip a candy/deep-fry thermometer to the side to provide accurate readings. Also you might need to raise the heat when adding food to compensate for the cooling of the oil, lowering it again as the oil returns to the proper frying temperature. An electric deep fryer has a thermostat that automatically adjusts the heat to maintain the selected temperature.

Remember, regardless of the method you use, not to fry too many pieces of fish at a time, which will cause the temperature of the oil to drop precipitously. Low frying temperatures will result in grease-sodden food.

Canola oil is my choice for deep-frying, as well as for general frying. It adds no flavor of its own and has a high smoke point of 450°F, well above the frying temperature of 360°F. In contrast, the smoke points of other popular fish-frying mediums can vary considerably. Lard, for example, begins to smoke between 360°F and 400°F, and vegetable shortening does so between 375°F and 425°F.

For complete directions for frying fish over an open fire, see "Canoe Country Fish Cookery" on page 28 and "How to Make an Authentic Guide's Shore Lunch" on page 40.

Panfrying

Use this method with walleye, bass, northern pike, panfish, catfish, and whitefish fillets. My first choice for this job is a cast-iron skillet, although any heavy bottomed skillet will do nicely.

Panfried Fish Fillets

Pour a layer of vegetable oil, shortening, or bacon grease about ⅛ to ¼ inch deep into the skillet and heat over medium heat until a drop of water dropped into the grease spits and sizzles. Bread the fish fillets with any of the breadings on pages 208 to 210 (save the batters for deep-frying). If you're in a hurry, simply season the fillets with salt and pepper and dredge in plain flour. Shake off the excess and lay the fillets with the flesh side down in the hot grease. Do not crowd the pan or the fish will steam, rather than brown properly. Use a long slotted spatula to turn the fish when golden brown. Continue frying until just cooked through. Drain on paper towels and serve immediately.

Fish may be panfried in butter, which gives them great flavor, but be sure to fry them at a lower temperature to avoid burning the butter.

Grilling

Grilling is suitable for any game fish fillets. Fish such as salmon and lake trout are excellent choices owing to their somewhat oilier flesh. Walleye and other delicate fish are difficult to grill because they tend to fall apart, but with a grill made especially for fish, it is easy and the results are delicious. Such grills, which sit on top of your regular barbecue grill, are available from many stores or can be purchased by mail order. You can marinate the fish before grilling (see Campfire-Grilled Game Fish Fillets, p. 34) or grill them plain. Fish may be grilled over a charcoal or wood fire.

Basic Grilled Fish Fillets

Spray the grilling surface with nonstick cooking spray and place it on the grill over hot coals or on a gas grill set on high. Brush the fillets lightly with olive oil or vegetable oil and season to taste with salt and pepper. Lay skin side up on the hot grill screen. When about half cooked, turn carefully with a flat spatula and finish grilling. Just before serving, brush the fish with melted butter or lemon butter if desired.

Grilled Whole Stream Trout

Plan on one whole trout per person. Gut and gill the trout, leaving the head on or not as you prefer. Wash the skin of the trout to remove as much of the slime as you can to help prevent sticking to the grill. Season the cavity with salt and freshly ground black pepper. Rub the skin of the trout lightly with vegetable oil and score the skin on both sides with a knife to reduce curling. Grill the trout on an oiled grill set close to white-hot coals for approximately 5 minutes per side. The skin will get too charred to eat, but the flesh inside will be moist and succulent and taste of the fire. You may baste the trout with butter while they grill if you like. Serve with lemon wedges or one of the compound butters on page 228.

Grinding or Chopping

Use this method with any game fish. Fish can be ground or chopped to make savory fish cakes and delicate sausages. See recipes for Walleye and Pistachio Nut Sausage, page 90; Lake Trout and Wild Rice Sausage with Morel Mushroom Sauce, page 93; Wilderness Walleye and Shrimp Croquettes with Horseradish Tartar Sauce and Northwoods Dressed Greens, page 84; and Lake Superior Salmon Cakes, page 98.

The Ten-Minute Rule for Cooking Fish

The ten-minute rule for cooking fish is often referred to as the Canadian rule, as it was developed in Canada. While not foolproof, the rule provides an excellent guide for timing the baking, roasting, broiling, and grilling of fish using high heat. Oven temperature should be set at 450°F.

Use a ruler to measure the fish at the thickest part. For every inch of thickness, the fish needs to be cooked for 10 minutes. That means if the fish were 1½ inches thick, you would cook it for 15 minutes. Stuffing a whole fish will increase the roasting time a little; add 5 minutes or so.

Remember this is only a guide, not a hard-and-fast rule. Use common sense and check frequently for proper doneness to avoid over- or undercooking.

Pickling

Northern pike is especially good for pickling. This recipe for pickled northern pike is from *The Gunflint Lodge Cookbook.*

Pickled Northern Pike

This is *good* pickled fish! Just be sure to let everything "age" in your refrigerator for at least 5 days before sampling and your patience will be well rewarded. It takes several days to put everything together, plus the aforementioned "aging" period. And don't worry about the bones in the northern pike; they are so softened by the pickling process you will never notice them. The spices and the sugar may be adjusted to suit your taste, and pimento pieces may be added for color. This recipe may be doubled. Serve with crackers for a great appetizer.

> 1 cup white vinegar
> ¾ cup white sugar
> 2 bay leaves
> 3 whole cloves
> ½ teaspoon whole allspice
> 1 teaspoon whole mustard seed
> ½ teaspoon whole black peppercorns
> ½ cup Silver Satin brand sweet white wine
> 1 cup pickling salt
> 2 quarts cold water
> 1 to 1½ pounds skinless northern pike, walleye, or any freshwater game
>   fish with rib bones removed, cut into 1-inch pieces
> 1½ to 2 cups additional white vinegar
> 1 medium onion, thinly sliced
> ½ lemon, thinly sliced

Day one: Combine the white vinegar, sugar, bay leaves, cloves, all-spice, mustard seed, and peppercorns in a nonreactive saucepan set over high heat. Bring to a boil, then reduce heat and simmer for 5 minutes. Cool slightly and add the sweet white wine. Pour the pickling syrup into a plastic or glass container, cover tightly, and let sit at room temperature for 4 days to allow flavors to mingle.

Mix the cup of salt with the cold water and stir thoroughly to dissolve salt. Pour over the cut-up skinless fish, cover, and refrigerate for 48 hours.

Day three: Drain the fish and rinse with cold water. Cover the fish with the white vinegar, cover, and refrigerate for 24 hours.

Day four: Drain the fish and discard vinegar, but do *not* rinse. Layer fish, sliced onions, and lemons in one or more glass or plastic containers. Do not pack too tightly. Cover with the pickling syrup. Cover tightly and refrigerate for at least 5 days, stirring fish at least once. Store in refrigerator covered with the pickling syrup for up to 6 weeks.

Planking

Planking is an easy and unique method of preparing large fish fillets for a crowd by roasting the fish on a board in front of the coals of a campfire. See "Planked Fish," page 50, for complete instructions.

Poaching

Best for lake trout, salmon, and whitefish, poaching is slow cooking in a liquid. In the classic method, the fish is put into cold liquid that is brought to the barest simmer over medium-low heat. The heat is then turned to very low and the fish is allowed to poach for about 10 minutes per inch of thickness at the thickest point. The liquid can be as simple as plain water or as elegant as the classic French "short broth," or Court Bouillon (p. 217), a simple vegetable broth made with water and a little vinegar or lemon juice.

Whole fish such as lake trout, salmon, and northern pike can be poached, but they require a special poaching pan long enough to accommodate a good-sized fish. The fish is wrapped in cheesecloth before poaching so it can be removed from the liquid without falling apart.

A classic preparation of the Anjou and Nantes regions of France is a whole northern pike poached in a Court Bouillon, then served with Beurre Nantais (p. 236), an exquisitely delicate butter sauce made with white wine vinegar and fish fumet.

Simple sauces for poached fish include a lemony homemade mayonnaise, a simple drawn butter, and lemon wedges, or even a salsa that is high in flavor yet low in fat.

Below is a variation on the classic method of poaching. It eliminates the problem of overcooking. This method works for fillets up to ¾ inch thick.

Basic Poached Fish Fillets

Fill a large skillet or saucepan with about 1½ to 2 inches of one of the following poaching mixtures: Court Bouillon; equal parts fish stock, water, and white wine; or 3 parts dry white wine, 1 part clam juice, and 2 parts water. Bring to a boil. Place serving-sized pieces of fish in the boiling water, cover the pan, and turn off the heat. Let sit for five minutes. Remove from water and serve.

Roasting

This method works well with all fish fillets and with whole fish. Roasting is done at high heat (450°F or more) with little or no added liquid.

Roasted Whole Fish

Preheat oven to 450°F. Brush prepared fish inside and out with lemon butter and season with salt and pepper. The head may be left on or not, depending on aesthetics and pan size. The fish may also be stuffed if desired. Place on a sheet pan or in a shallow casserole dish. Now this is the secret for baking to perfection every time: for each inch of fish thickness (when measured at the thickest part) bake in a preheated 450°F oven for 10 minutes. Thus a 1½-inch thick fish would need to bake for 15 minutes.

Roasted Fish Fillets

For this recipe, use fillets from salmon, lake trout, northern pike, muskellunge, or walleye. Preheat oven to 450°F. To roast one or two servings, use a pie tin; when cooking up several fillets, a shallow-sided sheet pan works best. Cut the fillets into serving-sized pieces. Spray the roasting pan with nonstick cooking spray and lay the fillets skin side down in the pan. Brush the top of the fish with butter or lemon butter and season lightly with salt and freshly ground black pepper. Roast in preheated oven using the 10-minute rule described in the previous recipe.

Searing

Searing can be used with all fish fillets. Searing is similar to panfrying, but the frying is done in a minimum of oil and the fish is not breaded.

Basic Seared Fish Fillets

Heat a heavy-bottomed skillet coated with a thin layer of vegetable or olive oil over medium-high heat. Season the fillets with salt and pepper and fry until nicely browned. As with panfried fish, avoid crowding the pan. Turn the fillets and continue cooking until just cooked through.

See also Seared Whitefish with Tuscan White Beans, Spinach Salad, and Tomato-Chive Vinaigrette, page 144.

Smoking

Smoking works especially well for oilier fish such as salmon, lake trout, and whitefish. See chapter 7, "The Smoker," for complete instructions on smoking fish.

Chapter 2

Camp and Shore Cookery

I n 1974 I spent the first of many summers at my Seagull Lake cabin, which is located near the end of the Gunflint Trail in far northern Minnesota. I spent most of that summer in a canoe and a tent, exploring the lakes and waterways of the Boundary Waters Canoe Area and Quetico Park along the Minnesota-Ontario border. In early June, a teacher friend and I completed the historic Hunter's Island route around the periphery of the Quetico. Many other trips followed and by the end of the summer, I had spent more nights in a tent than I had in my cabin.

I found it immensely enjoyable to cook over a campfire. Moreover, I found that preparing good food over an open fire depended more on what I packed than on the actual cooking. With a good cook kit and a reflector oven, I could cook almost anything I could make in my own kitchen.

The following summer I was hired as a fishing guide by Don Enzenauer at Voyageur Canoe Outfitters, located on the Seagull River. For the next seventeen summers I guided fishermen on lakes located on the Minnesota-Ontario border. It was here that I was able to combine my two passions: fishing and cooking. I took great pride in my shore lunches, which I would prepare from the morning catch.

Over time my campfire shore cuisine became more creative. I liked to surprise my clients with appetizers of my home-smoked trout and crackers with Chive-Horseradish Sauce (p. 223), deep-fried mushrooms (p. 46), or beer-batter fried onion rings (p. 46). With the fish, which I would also fry in beer batter or bread with pecans, I would serve wild rice pilaf, roasted sweet corn, and cornbread baked in a reflector oven or warm homemade rolls accompanied by homemade wild berry jams. There were even a few times when I baked a cake in the reflector oven for a client's birthday.

In this chapter you will discover the secrets to cooking over an open fire and learn a number of ways to cook fish in the backcountry. You will also learn how to prepare an authentic fishing guide's shore lunch and how to cook fish on a cedar plank, either in front of a fire or in your oven.

Canoe Country Fish Cookery

Catching fish and eating them while on a wilderness canoe trip is as close as any of us are likely to come to "living off the land." Temper such dreams with caution, however, and plan your menu as though fish had just become extinct. Some friends of mine packed light for a recent canoe trip through what they considered prime fishing country, expecting to eat fish for several meals. The fish didn't bite and they spent the last two days of their outing paddling back on short rations.

Sadly enough, they might have had all the fish they needed, had they only heeded the four easy steps to unparalleled fishing success, which I call "The Compleat Fishing Guide's Universal Fishing Primer":

1. Think positively.
2. Fish where the fish are.
3. Fish when the fish are hungry.
4. Fish with something the fish are hungry for.

At any rate, once you've caught some fish the rest of what follows will take on some significance.

Keeping Your Catch Fresh in Canoe Country

When fish die, they begin to deteriorate (a genteel word for rot) immediately. The colder you can keep the fish, the more that inevitable process can be slowed down. Packing fish in ice right after catching them is one of the best ways to do this. But, of course, this is out of the question in all but the fringes of canoe country.

Attempting to keep fish alive on stringers works for only a short while and in the warm surface water, the fish are soon floating belly up. The fine meal you anticipated is well on its way to being ruined.

So what can you do to keep fish fresh in the wilderness until you are ready to cook them? Eat them soon after catching them and take a tip from the old-time fishing guides who often had no access to ice. Instead of a stringer they carried a gunnysack and the fish they caught were immediately killed and put into it. The sack was then dipped in the lake and placed under the boat seat out of the sun. The bag was kept wet and evaporation kept the catch cool.

When in camp, the bag can be hung from a tree in a shaded spot, preferably in a good breeze. Keep the bag wet and your fish should remain in good eating condition for a few extra hours, depending on how warm and windy it is.

By the way, the gunnysack also makes a dandy lightweight canoe anchor. Simply put a few rocks in it and tie on a length of rope.

Backcountry Fish Fry

As a guide preparing shore lunches, I soon discovered that a hot campfire was the key to frying fish. Cook over a lively fire, not coals.

In a skillet, heat about ½ to ¾ inch of vegetable oil, lard, bacon grease, or a combination until hot but not smoking. While the grease is heating, bread the fillets using your favorite breading or one of the breadings listed on pages 208 to 210.

When the grease is the right temperature, the fish will turn a crisp golden brown at just about the same time they finish cooking. This is not as difficult to accomplish as it seems. Test the temperature of the grease by dipping the tail of a breaded fillet into it. If the grease sizzles and bubbles vigorously around the fish, the temperature is correct. Carefully place the fillets in the hot grease with the skin side down to minimize curling.

If the grease starts to smoke at any time before you start frying the fish it has gotten too hot. Remove the pan from the fire (carefully—spilled hot grease will flare up) and let cool a bit before proceeding.

A long-handled fork such as one used for hot dogs is the best utensil I have found for frying fish over an open fire. With it you can turn the fish without splashing the grease or singeing all the hair off your arm (a peculiar mark of pride among some guides I know). It can also tell you when the fish is done (the fork goes through the fillet easily), and the fork makes it easy to remove the crisp fillets to paper towels to drain.

Mix your breading before you go and pack it into plastic bags. Make sure the fillets are wet before shaking them in the breading bag in order to get a good coating.

Wilderness Cocktail Sauce

This sauce originated during a youthful stint as a fry cook. A customer insisted on having cocktail sauce with his deep-fried shrimp even after being told that there was none. Lacking the horseradish to make more I improvised, substituting Parmesan cheese for the horseradish. The customer said it was the best cocktail sauce he had ever tasted.

This sauce is excellent with any fried fish, but it is especially good with fish fillets cut into finger-sized strips, breaded, and deep-fried until golden brown. Eat them out of hand as you would shrimp, dipping the crisp morsels into the sauce.

> ½ cup ketchup
> 1 tablespoon grated Parmesan cheese
> Lemon juice to taste
> Cayenne pepper or hot pepper sauce to taste

Combine all ingredients and mix well. If Worcestershire sauce is a regular part of your seasoning kit, by all means add a few drops.

The Best Revenge

I am a firm believer in living comfortably and eating well while traveling in the backcountry. An old woodsman once said, "Roughin' it's for them that don't know no better." Heeding this admonishment, I always pack in a few "luxury" items such as a fresh lemon, an onion or two, and a small container of Dijon mustard. You'll need them for the following recipes. A fresh lemon once came in mighty handy on a recent trip to the Quetico when a canoe mate surprised us with a wineskin full of tequila as we sat around our evening fire.

Walleye Meuniere

This classic French dish is easily prepared over an open fire. No measurements are necessary as you will discover upon reading the recipe. I recommend using fresh lemon juice, but one of the small yellow plastic containers of the reconstituted will suffice. Any fish fillets or even small whole trout can be used for this recipe.

> Fish fillets
> Salt and pepper to taste
> Flour
> Vegetable oil or shortening
> Fresh or reconstituted lemon juice
> Dried parsley (optional)
> Butter or margarine

Heat about ⅛ inch of vegetable oil or shortening in a skillet until hot. Season fish fillets lightly with salt and pepper, dredge in flour to coat and shake off the excess. Place the fish in the pan with the skin side up. Fry until nicely browned and turn carefully with a spatula. When done, remove fillets to serving plates. Sprinkle each browned fillet lightly with lemon juice to taste and sprinkle with the dried parsley if you have it. Discard remaining fat and put in a tablespoon of butter or margarine for each fillet; when sizzling and light brown, pour the butter over the fish. Serve immediately.

Lake Trout Dijon

Imagine a freshly caught lake trout baked in foil with mustard and onions in its own juices. Be sure to use Dijon mustard, not the ballpark variety of yellow mustard. This recipe is also excellent with northern pike. Leave no trace—pack out your used foil.

Lake trout fillets, cut into serving-size pieces
Dijon mustard
Salt and pepper to taste
Lemon juice to taste (fresh or reconstituted)
Chopped fresh onion (reconstituted dried may be substituted, but the
      flavor will be quite different)
Melted butter or margarine
Aluminum foil

A Day in the Life of a Wilderness Fishing Guide

If you think fishing guides are bandits, lucky folks who are having too much fun to deserve to be paid, then this account of one day in late June on Saganaga Lake on the Minnesota-Ontario border might help to set the record straight.

There are five of us in my party today and we leave in two boats. Although still very overcast, the howling frigid winds out of the northwest that had pounded us for the last two days have at last died down and switched to a light breeze out of the southeast, bringing with it temperatures in the mid-sixties, a welcome change from the low fifties of the last few days.

We pass through Canadian customs six miles up the lake and head for the Northern Lights Lake portage on the far northeast arm of Saganaga Lake, another nine miles. At the portage we carry all of our gear, including motors and gas tanks, to boats we have cached on the other side. It is not long after we start fishing in our first spot that rain begins to pour down in sheets, with much cracking and crashing of thunder and lightning. We divide our time hunkering down on shore and fishing. The fishing is surprisingly good.

Luckily the rain stops long enough around noon to make shore lunch. An old beaver lodge yields wood that, while wet on the outside, is bone dry inside. While slicing an onion I slip with my fillet knife and take a thick slice off the end of my thumb. I have no bandages, so I use paper towels to staunch the bleeding. Later they become soaked in the continuing rain and fall apart. For the rest of the afternoon the

For each serving fold a large piece of aluminum foil in half. Smear a little of the melted butter on the foil and place a piece of trout skin side down in the center. Spread the top of the fillet liberally with the mustard. Season with salt, pepper, and drops of lemon juice. Sprinkle a layer of the chopped onions over the mustard and then drizzle with melted butter. Fold the edges of the foil over several turns to seal tightly.

Place the foil packages on top of the grill over hot coals. Add a few kindling-sized sticks of wood occasionally to maintain a steady temperature. Turn the packages every 5 minutes, being careful not to rip the foil. After 10 or 15 minutes, check one of the packages for doneness with a thinly sharpened stick. If the stick penetrates the fish easily, it is done. Open the packages carefully and eat right out of the foil or transfer fish to plates and pour the cooking juices over the top.

blood drips onto the bottom of the boat. Reeling in fish, netting them, baiting hooks, and running the motor are all painful endeavors as I keep bumping my thumb.

At 3:30 P.M. we start back to the portage. An intense thunderstorm forces us to once again take refuge on an island. For over a half hour lightning flashes, thunder booms, and rain pours. When we finally reach the portage we find Gordy Poehls, another guide, with motor trouble. He and his client had paddled their boat two miles to reach the portage. They are very lucky. Had we not stopped to wait out the last storm, we would have already been gone and we were the last boat back over. He will need to be towed in.

"Maybe we should wait for a break in the weather," I say to Gordy.

Gordy casts an experienced eye toward the sky. "It'll probably be dark before that happens."

I am not liking what I know has to be done. I will tow Gordy's boat behind mine. We will put as many people in my tag boat as we dare in order to make better time. As we head out from the portage another vigorous thunderstorm begins. Gordy sits nonchalantly in the back of his boat bailing out water as lightning strikes all around, some sounding far too close for comfort. It is a very slow trip and a frightening one. It rains so hard I have trouble seeing the shore. The usual forty-minute run back to the outfitter's dock stretches to nearly two hours. I find out later that well over three inches of rain had fallen.

Backcountry Mojakka

Here is a backcountry version of the traditional Finnish fish chowder, pronounced muy-YAK-ka. This is a good recipe to use when few fish have been caught and many are hungry. Another recipe for this soup using fresh ingredients can be found on page 59.

Bring 8 cups of water, 1 cup of diced fresh onions (or the equivalent of dried) and 1½ teaspoons of salt to a boil. Add one 6-ounce box of dried hash brown potatoes. Cover and set off to the side of the fire for 10 minutes. Slowly stir in 1 cup of dry milk powder and bring to a boil. Add as many boneless fish fillets cut up into 1-inch pieces as you want and 4 tablespoons of butter or margarine. Cover the pan and remove from heat. Let stand for 10 minutes beside the fire. Season to taste with salt and plenty of pepper and serve. This is mighty good served with oyster crackers and a shake or two of hot pepper sauce if you have it. Serves 6.

Campfire-Grilled Game Fish Fillets

This is a delicious and easy way to prepare freshly caught fish over a campfire. The fillets are briefly marinated in a flavor-enhancing vinaigrette before being grilled to smoky perfection over the coals of a campfire. In a pinch, a good Italian dressing from either a dry mix or a bottle may be substituted for the homemade vinaigrettes below. Use a folding fish grill for worry-free turning of fragile fillets. A charcoal fire can easily be substituted for a campfire. Accompany this with sweet corn grilled in the husks (p. 52), Smoky Chile BBQ Beans (p. 192), or Pepper Parmesan Potato Salad (p. 190), and some good bread for a most memorable shore feast.

> 2½ pounds skinless fish fillets, cut into serving-size pieces
> 1 to 1½ cups vinaigrette, as needed (recipes follow)
> Salt and freshly ground black pepper to taste

Place fish fillet pieces into a zipper-top plastic bag and pour dressing over the fish. Seal bag and place in the refrigerator or cooler to marinate for 30 minutes to 1 hour.

Spray a folding fish grill or grill screen with nonstick cooking spray. Remove fish from vinaigrette and place on grill, seasoning lightly with salt and pepper. Grill over a hot campfire that is mostly coals or over a charcoal fire, turning once and basting once or twice with vinaigrette until fish is just barely done. Serve at once. Serves 6.

Basic Vinaigrette

This vinaigrette may be varied in numerous ways. For an herb vinaigrette, add about ⅓ cup fresh herbs such as basil, chives, parsley, dill or thyme, alone or in combination. A nice lemon-caper variety may be made by making the vinaigrette with lemon juice and adding about a tablespoon of chopped capers and a bit of grated lemon zest.

> 1 clove garlic
> ½ teaspoon kosher salt
> 1 tablespoon minced shallot or onion
> 1 teaspoon Dijon mustard
> ¼ to ⅓ cup red wine vinegar or fresh lemon juice
> 1 cup extra-virgin olive oil or vegetable oil
> Salt and freshly ground black pepper to taste

Chop and mash together the garlic and salt to make a paste. Scrape up and place in a small bowl. Add the shallot or onion, the Dijon mustard, and the vinegar or lemon juice and whisk until well blended. Drizzle in the oil while whisking constantly. Season to taste with additional salt and pepper. Store in the refrigerator until needed.

Asian Vinaigrette

This is especially nice with northern pike, lake trout, or salmon.

1½ teaspoons finely chopped shallots
½ teaspoon finely chopped fresh ginger
½ teaspoon finely minced garlic
¼ cup soy sauce
¼ cup freshly squeezed lime juice
½ cup peanut or vegetable oil
2¼ teaspoons Oriental sesame oil
2 tablespoons sugar
1½ teaspoons chile paste with garlic (more to taste!)

Combine all ingredients and whisk together until well mixed.
Refrigerate until needed.

Vinaigrettes are best stored in a jar with a tight lid so they can be shaken vigorously to recombine.

Campfire Cookery Wisdom

For some reason cooking over an open fire seems to have a numbing effect on the minds of otherwise intelligent people. In a home kitchen no one would ever wonder why their eggs, for example, were starting to burn if the pan was set on a red hot burner. But put them in front of a campfire and there they'll be, with flames leaping all around their pans, wondering why everything they cook seems to burn so easily. It's all a matter of common sense.

First make sure you have plenty of dry firewood of all different sizes. Small dry wood burns quickly, creating fast hot heat for sautéing; larger pieces burn more slowly for stewing or simmering. Start your fire well before dinner and allow it to burn down to a good set of coals with only a few flames visible. A hot bed of coals is the ticket. Add wood sparingly to the bed of coals to create and maintain the correct cooking temperature. By moving pans to different places around the fire grate, you can vary the cooking temperature considerably. Pans may even be set beside the fire to keep warm. Propping a pan up at an angle to the fire works like a broiler and lets you brown the top of a gratin or a bannock.

One final tip: put your dishwater on to heat when your fire is getting started, then remove it while cooking. The water will remain warm. Replace the dishwater while eating and add additional wood. Your dishwater will be ready to use right after dinner.

The Wilderness Chef's Seasoning Kit

Putting together an all-purpose seasoning kit will make your camp-fire cuisine more memorable. Amounts should be based on anticipated use. (You will use a lot more salt than cayenne pepper for example.) Personalize your kit by leaving out what you will not use, such as the cayenne or hot pepper sauce, for example, if you're not into spicy foods.

Pack your seasonings in small plastic bags, 35mm film canisters, or, best of all, small plastic screw-top bottles (some even come with pour-and-shake openings; you can also recycle seasoning containers from the store). Pack in a larger plastic container with a tight lid to keep the kit together and handy to use. A week in the wilderness doesn't have to mean a week in culinary purgatory.

The Basics

Salt—kosher or iodized

Black pepper (I take along a small pepper grinder.)

Lemon pepper seasoning

Seasoned salt (Your favorite brand or your own concoction. My Gunflint Steak and Chop Seasoning is on page 39 and Ron Berg's Game Fish Seasoning is on page 211.)

Cayenne (ground red pepper)

Curry powder

Thyme

Basil

Oregano

Paprika—Invaluable in making fish breadings.

Fresh garlic—Keeps well, weighs little. Why use powder?

Dried onions—In addition, I always pack at least one fresh onion.

Optional—Great flavor boosters

Hot pepper sauce—Spices up eggs and soups.
Worcestershire sauce—Adds flavor to meats, soups, and stews.
Fresh lemon—You can substitute a plastic lemon, but there's no
advantage in either weight or flavor.

Transfer the first two items to miniature squeeze bottles or small
plastic bottles with tight-fitting lids.

Optional—Adds a gourmet touch to many dishes

Follow package directions for soaking and using the first two items.
In some cases the soaking juices are used as well.

Dried tomatoes—Add to rice dishes, soups, eggs, stews, or couscous.
Dried wild mushrooms—Great in scrambled eggs or added to stews or
soups.
Fresh Parmesan cheese—Grate and pack in zipper-top bags just before
leaving to preserve freshness. Excellent on eggs, vegetables, pasta, rice
dishes.

Gunflint Steak and Chop Seasoning

2 cups kosher salt
3 tablespoons granulated garlic
2 tablespoons lemon pepper seasoning
2 tablespoons celery salt
2 tablespoons onion powder
1 tablespoon plus 1 teaspoon Cajun seasoning (such as Paul Prudhomme's
Cajun Magic®)
1 teaspoon cornstarch

Combine all ingredients and mix well.

How to Make an Authentic Guide's Shore Lunch

Shore lunch brings to mind images of sparkling blue northern lakes, the smell of wood smoke and pine, and, without a doubt, absolutely the best fish you've ever eaten. It's a humble meal—fried fish, freshly caught, served up with fried potatoes and beans, washed down with black coffee and topped off with an apple or an orange if you remembered to pack them. You can even do it at home if you don't mind the mess, but it is best made over an open fire. In a pinch you can make one on a two-burner gas camp stove, which guides have to use during open-fire bans.

If you've ever hired a guide and opted for a shore lunch, you certainly remember how wonderful everything tasted. Why not put one together yourself on your next fishing trip? It's not hard to do if you do some advance planning.

Here is a shore lunch menu typical of the ones prepared all over the north:

> Crisp Golden-Fried Freshly Caught Fish
>   (If not available, see "Dreaded Plan B" on p. 45.)
> Fried Potatoes and Onions
> Pork and Beans
> Bread and Butter
> Cookies or Fruit
> Guide's Campfire Coffee

Here's what you need to pack:

> 1 10- to 14-inch skillet, depending on how many hungry fishermen you
>   have to feed. A long-handled 14-inch pan will feed a crowd.
> 2 saucepans—1-quart and 2-quart
> 1 2-quart coffeepot

2 pie tins (for fillets or breading)

Enough shortening, vegetable oil, lard, or bacon grease, alone or in combination, to fill your skillet about half full

1 whole cooked potato per person

Canned pork and beans, your favorite brand. Figure on about two to three servings per can (or Smoky Chile BBQ Beans, p. 192).

2 slices for each person of buttered bread, or bread plus butter or margarine

Cookies, fruit, or other choice for dessert

1 or 2 large onions

Salt and pepper

Coffee—I soon learned to pack double coffee in case I spilled a pot or had to brew another.

Eating utensils

Paper plates

Paper towels

Paper or foam cups

Fish breading—Choose one from chapter 9 or one of your favorites.

1 slotted spoon (to remove the fried potatoes and onions)

1 long-handled, long-tined fork (an old hot dog roasting fork works well)

1 scouring pad

1 hot pad, oven mitt, or old glove

Any additional ingredients or items from "Shore Lunch Additions and Dividends"

1 or 2 cans of Spam® or hash (see "Dreaded Plan B")

Boiled potatoes are strictly nontraditional. The traditional shore lunch potatoes are the little round canned variety. Having fried and eaten several thousand of these over a seventeen-year guiding career, I prefer the boiled potatoes. However, feel free to use the well-drained canned variety, either whole or sliced, if you prefer. Hash browns are also nice for a change, as is the Pepper Parmesan Potato Salad on page 190.

As you pull into shore after your successful morning on the water, everything you need for shore lunch is in your carefully packed wannigan, or packsack, and in your fish box. The fish box of today is likely to be a cooler with ice and not the burlap or moss-lined wooden boxes of yesteryear. Stringers and live wells do a poor job of keeping your fish in tip-top eating condition and are not recommended.

First, make sure that you have gathered plenty of dry wood if you are cooking over a campfire. There is nothing worse than having to run into the woods to look for more wood while your fish are lying in lukewarm shortening.

Build a lively fire and set the coffeepot full of water on the grate to boil while you (or preferably someone else) is cleaning the fish. After rinsing the fillets, check the coffeepot to see if the water is boiling. If it is, set it off to one side of the fire and add the coffee, about 6 to 8 heaping teaspoons for the 2-quart pot. Stir once and let brew beside the fire. Set a cook pot with the beans off to the side of the fire to begin heating. *Do not stir!* Stirring breaks them up and "ruins them" as a fellow guide once warned me as I was about to stick a spoon into his bean pot.

Now put the shortening into the skillet. The grease should come about half way to the top of the pan. Place the skillet over the hottest part of the fire. Also turn the beans a quarter turn as the side toward the fire starts to bubble.

While the shortening is heating, slice the cooked potatoes into ¼-inch thick slices (or drain the canned ones). Also peel the onion. (Don't forget to turn the beans another quarter turn.) Add wood to keep a lively fire going under the skillet.

Like the old Chicago ward boss's advice on voting, check the grease early and often. If it begins to smoke, the grease has gotten too hot. The only thing to do then is remove the pan from the fire and let it cool a bit before continuing. To see if the grease is hot enough, drop in a potato slice. If the grease bubbles and sizzles vigorously around it, it's time to add the potatoes. To prevent a flare-up from grease bubbling over the side onto the flames, remove the skillet from the grate and set it in a level spot. Carefully pour in the potatoes and return to the fire. (Turn the beans again.) Also this would be a good time to add about a ½ cup of cold water to the coffeepot to settle the grounds. Stir the pot gently with a clean stick or spoon after adding the water and let stand a few minutes. The coffee can now be served or set beside the fire to keep warm.

When the potatoes start to turn golden brown, slice the onion into thick ¼-inch slices and add to the potatoes. Stir occasionally to make sure everything browns evenly.

When the potatoes and onions are golden brown, remove them with the slotted spoon to one of the saucepans lined with several layers of paper towels. Set the pot with the potatoes near the fire to keep warm. (Watch the beans. If they're hot set them off to the side to keep warm.)

Add more wood to the fire under the skillet and bread the fish fillets. Dip the tail of one of the fillets into the pan to test the temperature. It should start to sizzle and bubble immediately. Guides and other old hands at shore lunches know to put the fillets into the grease with the skin side down to minimize curling. Use the long-handled fork to turn the fillets and to tell when they are done. The fork will easily go through the fillets when they are. Remove the fillets as they get done and drain on one of the pie tins lined with paper towels.

With experience, you will find that the fat has to be hotter for fillets breaded with flour and cornmeal than for those breaded with egg wash and cracker or bread crumbs in order for them to brown and cook properly.

When the last of the fish are cooked, the guide will carefully pour the hot grease on the fire (stand back!) and immediately dunk the hot frying pan in the lake. This makes cleaning it easier.

Time now to find a comfortable spot under a tall jack pine and enjoy one of the finest meals you will ever eat while looking out over the sparkling lake and perhaps contemplating where the big ones might be lurking after lunch. It just doesn't get any better than this.

Peril from Above

One lazy summer day a few years ago, I was enjoying a day off fishing with my friend and fellow fishing guide, Mike Wiest. We were anchored on a promising looking piece of Saganaga Lake structure slip-bobbering for walleyes. Suddenly Mike let loose with a string of epithets and curses that would have done any jack-pine savage proud. I glanced over to see him wiping what were obviously the fresh white droppings of a bird off his upper arm and pants leg. Immediately I looked up to spot the offending bird, but the sky was curiously empty of seagulls.

"I know," Mike snarled, washing himself off by the side of the boat. "I looked too. The son of a bitch must have been above the clouds!"

I later found out that this was not Mike's first encounter with a diarrhetic gull. Not only had a gull befouled him in a similar fashion on a previous occasion, he later admitted to an encounter with a Canadian goose while hunting. Mike said he had actually seen the approaching goose let loose with its cargo, but was so mesmerized by the sight of the fecal missile hurtling unerringly toward him that he neither shot at the goose, nor moved out of harm's way. He admitted that after wiping off his hunting jacket, he had gained a healthy respect for the tremendous amount of recycled corn a goose can release at one time.

Mike's sister suggested that such things might run in the Wiest family, as a robin flying overhead had once decorated her stomach while she lay sunning herself poolside.

This was all very curious, so to see what the odds were of this happening with any frequency, I polled a number of fishing guides who all together had accumulated a total of over sixty summers on the water. The results were unanimous. Never once had this happened to any of them, although Gordy Poehls told of an incident that happened once while he was making a shore lunch. It seems that a gull flying overhead had scored a direct hit on his frying pan, plopping with a splash into the grease that was full of frying fish fillets.

"Just hold on," he told his wide-eyed fishermen, "I can't do anything until it gets crisp enough to scoop it out." As Gordy recalled, most of the fish went uneaten.

Dreaded Plan B

Even the best of guides occasionally comes up short for lunch, hence the need for an alternative to freshly caught fish. Spam® and corned beef hash are the traditional northwoods substitutes and you'd be smart to pack one of these or a suitable alternative. If you will be fishing in the Boundary Waters Canoe Area Wilderness (BWCAW), where cans and bottles are not allowed, be sure to remove the faux fish from the cans and pack them into acceptable containers.

A Few Final Tips

In most areas you will need to pack a grate to cook on.

If you are short on fish and long on hungry fishermen, take a tip from one who has been there. Make a beer batter and cut the fish into finger-sized strips before battering and frying. The fish will go almost twice as far this way.

Flour-type breadings may be used again. Pack a clean plastic bag and transfer the breading to it after breading the fish. Back in camp or at home, shake it through a wire-mesh sieve to remove any lumps.

Make sure your campfire is dead out before you leave camp.

Leave no trace—pack out everything you can't burn.

Shore Lunch Additions and Dividends

Bacon

There are few things that have more affinity with the outdoors than bacon. The sweet smoky aromas of bacon frying over an open fire mingling with the smell of wood smoke is something you're not likely to forget. A fellow guide showed me this method of frying bacon one bone-numbing cold, rainy day in early June a few years back when we were guiding a party of fishermen together.

Take an entire pound of sliced bacon and carefully add it, unseparated, to the hot grease in your skillet before you add the potatoes. Use the long-handled fork to "shake" the bacon into individual slices as it fries. Remove to paper towels to drain when brown and crisp. The bacon cooks quickly without burning, and all the bacon fat is rendered out to flavor the potatoes and the fish when it's their turn in the pan.

Serve the crisp bacon as an appetizer or put aside to crumble over the potatoes before serving (or save a few slices for yourself to make the Guide's Deluxe Shore Lunch Walleye Sandwich, on p. 47).

Onion Rings

When time permits, onion rings are a delicious and easy addition to shore lunch. Use the same breading or batter you are using for the fish and deep-fry the breaded rings until golden crisp and brown. Serve as an appetizer or as an accompaniment to the fish.

Fried Mushrooms

Here's a real treat that will impress anyone who eats one of your shore lunches. Bread a pound or so of fresh mushrooms using any of the breadings. You might have to rinse the mushrooms with water to get the dry breadings to stick. Deep-fry until golden brown and serve as an appetizer.

The Guide's Deluxe Shore Lunch Walleye Sandwich

Place a hot, crisp, fried walleye fillet on a slice of bread, buttered or not as you prefer. Place a couple of thin slices of raw onion over the fish and finish with a crisp slice of bacon or two if you have them. Spoon on tartar sauce or top with what some guides call the tartar sauce of the northwoods—pork and beans—and cover everything with another slice of bread.

Kenora Fried Potatoes

One of my clients described to me how a guide who worked in the Kenora area in Canada prepared shore lunch potatoes. You'll need to pack an extra skillet to fry the fish if you decide to make these tasty campfire au gratins.

Dice or slice cold boiled potatoes and fry them in about ⅛ inch of your choice of shortening. Toss and turn until the potatoes begin to turn brown and crisp and are almost done. Now add as many diced onions and chopped green peppers as you like. Fry until the potatoes are nicely browned and the onions and peppers are tender. Season the whole thing with salt and pepper to taste. Lay slices of your favorite cheese—American, brick, cheddar, or jack to name a few—over the top of the potatoes and keep them warm beside the fire until the cheese is melted.

Shore Lunch Pommes Dauphine

These unusual potatoes were a hit on many of my shore lunches. A combination of mashed potatoes and cream-puff dough, these golf-ball-size potatoes fry up crisp and golden brown and are somewhat hollow inside. They lend themselves to many variations, some of which are listed below.

> ½ cup water
> ¼ cup butter
> 1 teaspoon salt
> ½ cup all-purpose flour
> 2 eggs
> 1½ cups warm seasoned mashed potatoes
>   (or equivalent in reconstituted instant mashed)
> Speck of nutmeg

In a small saucepan set over medium-high heat, bring water, butter, and salt to a rolling boil. Reduce heat to low and add the flour all at once, stirring vigorously until smooth and the dough leaves the sides of the pan and forms a ball (about 1 minute). Turn off heat and beat in the eggs, one at a time, beating the mixture until smooth and

Thunderstorms!

There is only one thing I truly fear when I'm out on the water—lightning. At the first sign of an approaching thunderstorm, I expeditiously head for shore with one exception: if I happen to be reasonably close to Powell's Chippewa Inn, I make that my destination, where good company, a pot of hot coffee, and an open porch on which to sit and watch the storm await. Many's the time when it seemed like every guide working the lake would show up at Powell's to sit out a storm. Once, during one vigorous thunderstorm that lasted well past the lunch hour, Dorothy Powell offered me the use of the inn's kitchen to make shore lunch for my clients.

And yet despite my fear, there were more foolish occasions than I care to remember when I tried to outrun a storm. These irrational races most often occurred near the end of the day, when all I wanted was to get back to the dock, clean my catch, and go home. It was foolish because the storms always moved faster than I could and doubly foolish because the leading edge of the storm often produces the worst lightning.

When I would prudently decide to take refuge on shore, I was careful to pick my velvety after each egg. Beat in the mashed potatoes and the nutmeg. *May be made ahead to this point and refrigerated for up to 24 hours.*

Deep-fry in 360°F oil by dropping rounded tablespoons or use a small (#50) cookie scoop (dip into the hot oil between scoops). Fry until puffed and golden on both sides. Drain on paper towels. Makes about 30, enough for 3 to 4 servings.

Optional Additions:

> Chopped parsley
> Minced onions
> Chopped chives
> Grated Parmesan
> Grated Swiss, cheddar, or other cheese
> Rutabagas (mashed with the potatoes)
> Bacon bits

Use a sturdy wooden spoon to do all the beating. A mixer with a paddle attachment makes quick work of beating in the eggs. Leftover mashed potatoes may be used if they are warmed in the microwave first.

---

spots. Over my years on the lake, I had observed that Norway pines, white pines, and jack pines were most often struck by lightning. On the other hand, I had seldom, if ever, seen a spruce, cedar, birch, or poplar tree that had been hit by lightning—not to say they never are. Lightning is much too capricious to make any assumptions about it. However, some faith is better than none, so I would take my refuge near those trees, favoring the shorter ones, of course.

Occasionally, the unpredictable nature of lightning is truly frightening. Several summers ago, two clients and I were fishing for lake trout on one of Saganaga's many trout reefs. It had been a calm sunny day with only a few scattered clouds. We noticed a large black cloud over the Canadian shore that appeared to be coming our way. We could see that it was raining quite heavily beneath it and we got into our raingear. While it was passing over us there was a sudden flash and an almost simultaneous crash of thunder. "Reel in!" I shouted, starting the motor and beginning to head for shore, even as we were still frantically reeling in our lines. There had been no warning, no previous strikes, just one rogue strike that seemed to barely miss us.

Planked Fish

Freshly caught fish baked on an aromatic plank in front of a camp-fire are a unique treat. The fish cooks up moist and succulent, tasting of both the fire and the plank. It is a great way to cook for a crowd and was a staple at the picnics put on by the fishing families of Minnesota's North Shore who summered on Isle Royale during the fishing season.

Planking is an easy way to cook larger fish, say three pounds or more. Although oilier fish such as lake trout, salmon, and steelhead are traditional, any species of fish can be planked. The fish may be individual fillets or whole fish that have been opened up like a book.

Native Americans who lived along the coasts in the Pacific Northwest and around the Great Lakes were probably the first ones to plank fish. The fish were most likely impaled on a stick or perhaps lashed to a split log with green branches. Today planked fish are usually nailed to the board (avoid galvanized nails). The fillets may also be "tied" to the board with wire.

The most commonly used wood is cedar, which imparts a subtle aromatic flavor to the cooked fish, but you can use any hardwood plank or even a split log when necessary. If the wood is green so much the better for the flavor it passes to the fish. The wood should be about 2 inches wider than the fillets.

To begin, build a fire well ahead of time and feed it often to build up a good deep bed of coals. When the fire is ready, brush the board with a little vegetable oil. If you have a favorite marinade, the fish may be marinated beforehand. Lay the fish fillet(s) skin side down on the board and nail the fish to the board. Brush the fish with melted butter, vegetable oil, or olive oil and season with salt and freshly ground black pepper. The butter or oil may be flavored with chopped garlic if desired. Fresh herbs such as chopped chives, dill, or parsley may be sprinkled on as well. Alternatively, strips of bacon may be tacked across the fish to provide continual basting and a different flavor.

Prop the fish on its board up before the bed of coals. Place the bottom of the plank about 5 inches away from the edge of the fire. Cooking time will vary depending on the thickness of the fillets. Continue cooking, basting occasionally (unless using bacon) and turning the board end for end once or twice, until most of the raw look is gone between the flakes of the thickest part of the fish, anywhere from 30 minutes to a couple of hours.

Use a spatula to serve the fish right from the plank. The skin will stick to the board. Best of all the cleanup is a snap—the plank is burned in the fire after dinner.

Corn on the cob roasted in their husks on top of the coals is a great accompaniment to the planked fish. Roast the ears on the coals of the fire as directed on page 52.

Planked Fish in the Oven

Fish may also be baked in your oven on an untreated cedar shake (shingle) or 1-by-6-inch board, or on special cedar planks that are manufactured for just such a task. These planks can often be purchased via mail order in the backs of cooking magazines. One shake or plank will usually hold enough fish for one or two servings. Cedar Planked Salmon is a specialty in some restaurants.

Preheat oven to 400°F. Lightly "toast" the cedar plank by placing it directly on the oven rack and baking for about 8 minutes. This "seasons" the plank by releasing some of the resins in the wood to flavor the fish.

Remove the plank from the oven and, while still hot, use a paper towel to rub a thin coating of olive or vegetable oil on the plank (this keeps the fish from sticking to the plank). Place the fish fillet, marinated if you like, skin side down on the hot plank. Brush the fish with butter, vegetable, or olive oil and season as needed with salt and freshly ground black pepper. Return to the oven and roast on the plank for 8 to 10 minutes or until the fish barely tests done.

To avoid dripping in the oven, the planks with the fish may be placed on sheet pans during baking. Serve the fish right on the plank or remove to a heated serving plate.

Campfire-Roasted Sweet Corn in Husks

After World War II, I lived for a few years at my great-grandfather's farm just outside Wayzata on old Highway 12, a few miles west of Minneapolis. Some of my earliest food memories date from that stay.

I remember going into the woods with my great-grandfather to cool, dense blackberry and gooseberry patches full of earthy fruity aromas where, amazingly to my young mind, good things to eat could be had just for the picking. I can still picture my great-grandmother sitting in the shade of the roofed porch of the three-story farmhouse, churning sweet cream butter with an old wooden churn. And I remember the simple savory flavors of sage, pork, liver, and cornmeal in the crisp slices of homemade scrapple she fried for breakfast. Ah, but most of all I remember the smoky caramelized flavors of roasted fresh sweet corn swathed in butter and seasoned with salt and pepper from a family corn roast on a long ago summer night in July when the first ears of corn had finally ripened.

As I recall, a large shallow fire pit was dug first and in it a hardwood fire was started in the afternoon and fed frequently to build up a good bed of coals. After evening chores, the coals were raked to one side and the ears of corn, picked only an hour or so earlier and still in their husks, were taken from the washtubs where they had been soaking in cold water and strewn over the hot ground. The coals were raked back over the corn and a large wet canvas tarp was laid over the top.

It was dusk by the time the tarp was removed, releasing bellows of smoke and steam. The ears of corn with their blackened husks were fished out of the fire pit with rakes and shovels. A pan of cold water was set close at hand. A plunge into the water cooled the cobs just enough to peel back the husks, revealing the steaming sweet yellow kernels tinged with specks of golden brown. Crocks of great-grandmother's homemade butter and shakers of salt and pepper were set out on an old wooden picnic table along with piles of napkins. More wood was now heaped on the coals and the leaping flames provided light and warmth for our task. Roasted corn was the only thing on the menu on that lazy July evening, and we feasted on it, eating cob after cob after cob, mindless of our soot- and butter-covered hands and faces.

Roasted corn is one of my favorite accompaniments to a campfire-prepared meal (and one of the easiest). Simply soak the corn in cold water for an hour or so, then place them directly on the hot coals (not flaming) and turn frequently until the husks are blackened and the corn is hot and flecked with spots of caramelized brown. The soaked corn may also be buried directly in the coals for about 10 minutes or so.

Sometimes instead of roasting corn in the ashes of a fire, I do it instead on a grate set over the coals of a campfire or on a charcoal grill. The corn needs to be soaked in cold water for 30 minutes to an hour before roasting, but don't worry about removing the silk before roasting since it comes off easily with the husks after the corn is cooked. If I'm having roasted corn with my shore lunch, I build a little rock corral on the shore and lay the corn in the water to soak while I'm getting the fire going.

To roast the corn, remove the cobs from the water and drain. Place on a grill over a medium wood or charcoal fire. If using a covered grill, replace the cover. Turn the cobs as the husks become charred. The husks will look quite burned, but the corn will remain moist beneath. Ideally when done, the tops of some of the kernels will be nicely browned and caramelized. The whole process will take 15 to 20 minutes or longer, depending on the heat of your fire.

And finally, here is an easy way to get butter on the corn. Fill a deep pot ½ to ¾ full of water and place a half to a full pound of butter in the water. Heat the water until the butter melts and floats on top of the water. Peel the husk on the corn all the way back. Using the husk as a handle, dip the corn down through the butter into the water and back up. The corn is now buttered. Serve with salt and pepper and lots of napkins.

Chapter 3

Fishing Camp and Cabin Recipes

he recipes in this chapter all have one thing in common: they are quick and easy to prepare at your fishing camp or cabin with a minimum of ingredients or with ingredients that can be easily purchased while traveling.

In any case it is a good idea to plan ahead. Make a menu of the meals you plan to make and a list of all the ingredients you will need. That way you will not only avoid packing unnecessary ingredients, but also ensure that you will not forget anything essential. If you plan to eat the fish you catch, include them on your menus, but be sure to pack an alternative in case the fish are not biting.

When I plan on cooking away from home, I always pack several useful items. One is a good chef's knife, as good knives of any sort are rarely available no matter where I stay. I have a small 6-inch chef's knife that works well and packs easily, but an 8-inch knife will do just fine. Also essential, I believe, is a pocketknife with a sharp blade. It does the work of a paring knife, serves as a fine steak knife, and has other uses too numerous to mention.

Other items I find indispensable and rarely available are a good vegetable peeler, a decent corkscrew, and a pepper mill (don't forget extra peppercorns). All can be rolled up in a heavy towel and packed in your pack or suitcase. (If you are flying, make sure you pack your chef's knife in the luggage you check through and *not* in your carry-on luggage.)

And finally, if I plan to drink wine with my meals, I bring some fairly cheap wine glasses (well packed, of course) or some of the better quality plastic ones. I have never enjoyed drinking wine out of paper cups or the jelly jars that often passed for glasses in many of the small resorts I used to frequent.

The Great Minnesota Fishing Camp Breakfast

Minnesota's anglers are a hearty breed who endure wind, freezing rain, and burning sun without complaint to enjoy the sport of fishing and good fellowship. They fish hard, play cards late, get up early, and tell lies . . . expertly. They also know how to eat well wherever they make their camps.

The menu that follows makes use of much of the bounty of Minnesota's woods and waters. Freshly caught, crisply fried fish are paired with scrambled eggs, a match made in heaven. Minnesota wild rice has been added to the eggs along with diced red peppers, sliced fresh mushrooms, and the tangy richness of cream cheese. The melt-in-your-mouth corn muffins with butter and honey, also a natural with fish, add incomparable luxury. This is the angler's reward for a good catch and it is worth the extra time to be able to start at least one day of our lives with such a fine beginning.

Golden Fried Fillets of Minnesota Game Fish

There is no doubt that fresh fish tastes considerably better than frozen. However, frozen fish is better than none and may certainly be substituted for the fresh.

> 1½ pounds boneless game fish fillets, cut into 6 4-ounce portions
> ¾ cup Northwoods All-Purpose Breading Mix (p. 208)
> 1 egg beaten with ¼ cup of liquid—water, white wine, milk, evaporated milk, cream, or beer
> 1½ cups dry or fresh bread crumbs, crushed crackers, or cracker meal
> Vegetable oil or shortening, as needed for frying

Put the Northwoods All-Purpose Breading Mix in a paper or plastic bag. Place both the egg mixture and the bread crumbs into separate flat pans, such as pie tins. Shake fish fillets in the bag containing the breading mix. Shake off the excess, then dip into the egg mixture, and finally into the bread crumbs, using your hand to coat the fish.

Bread all the fish and lay them in a single layer on a platter or pan. Although not absolutely necessary, refrigerating the breaded fillets for 30 minutes or so not only allows the breading to set up, but will give you time to attend to the muffins and eggs.

To fry the fish, heat about ½ inch of vegetable oil or shortening in a 10-inch skillet over medium-high heat. When hot but not smoking, add the fish fillets and fry, turning once, until golden brown on both sides. If necessary fry in 2 batches. Drain on paper towels and keep warm, uncovered, in a low (150°F) oven. Makes 6 4-ounce servings.

Scrambled Eggs with Wild Rice, Shiitake Mushrooms, and Red Peppers

If you prefer, 4 ounces of shredded Monterey Jack or other cheese may be substituted for the cream cheese.

> 4 tablespoons butter
> 4 ounces fresh shiitake mushrooms or 8 ounces thinly sliced white
>   mushrooms or a combination
> 6 tablespoons finely chopped onions or green onions
> 12 large eggs, beaten lightly in a large bowl with ¾ teaspoon salt and
>   several shakes of hot pepper sauce
> ¾ cup cooked wild rice (about ¼ cup uncooked)
> 3 tablespoons finely diced red pepper (or substitute green pepper)
> 3 ounces cream cheese, cut into ½-inch cubes
> Chopped parsley, snipped chives, or sliced green onion tops for garnish

In a 10-inch skillet (nonstick preferred), melt the butter over medium-high heat. When the butter is sizzling, add the sliced mushrooms and toss and turn for about a minute. Add the onions and stir until transparent. Add the eggs and cook, lifting, turning, and gently chopping the eggs with a wide spatula. When the eggs are soft-set, stir in the wild rice, the red peppers, and the cream cheese. Cook until cream cheese is mostly incorporated and the eggs are heated through. Scrape into a heated serving dish and sprinkle with parsley, chives, or green onion tops. Serves 6.

Featherlight Corn Muffins

As with all muffins, a light hand ensures light results. Consequently, muffin ingredients are never beaten. Stir the ingredients together until just combined. Heavy muffins are not appreciated by anyone, not even starving fishermen.

> 1 cup all-purpose flour
> ½ cup yellow stone-ground cornmeal
> ¼ cup sugar
> 1½ teaspoons baking powder
> ¼ teaspoon salt
> 2 large eggs
> ¼ cup milk
> ½ cup (1 stick) butter, melted and cooled

Preheat the oven to 350°F. In a bowl sift together the flour, cornmeal, sugar, baking powder, and salt. *(May be made ahead and packed in a plastic bag until needed.)* In another bowl, beat the eggs with the milk. Add the flour-cornmeal mixture to the eggs and milk *alternately* with the melted and cooled butter. Mix only until the flour is barely incorporated. Spoon into 8 buttered and floured 2½-inch muffin tins. Bake for 15 to 20 minutes or until the muffins are nicely browned and a toothpick inserted into the muffins comes out clean. Serves 6 with 2 extra muffins to fight over.

Before You Go

Plan ahead and keep things simple.

For the fish:

1. Prepare Northwoods All-Purpose Breading Mix and pack in plastic bag.
2. Prepare bread crumbs or crush crackers and pack in plastic bag.

For the eggs:

1. Cook wild rice, cool, and pack in plastic bag. Refrigerate or freeze until needed.
2. Chop red peppers and refrigerate or freeze until needed.

For the muffins:

1. Sift together the dry ingredients and pack in a plastic bag.
2. Don't forget to pack the muffin tin.

Mojakka

The recipe for this traditional Finnish fish soup is recorded below exactly as received from "Wild Man" Dewey Pihlman at his hilltop estate on the Seagull River some years ago:

Boil potatoes, celery, onions, salt, pepper. Drain. Cover with milk, half-and-half, and ¼ pound butter and bring to a boil. Add walleye fillets as soon as it starts to boil hard. Cover and remove from heat.

His fair wife, Robin, recommends using only walleye for this soup, going so far as to claim that this soup isn't nearly as good when made with northern pike fillets.

Here is my rendition of Dewey's recipe, however, it should be noted that any way you put this together, the end result will be mojakka.

> 1 cup each potatoes, celery, and onions diced into ½-inch pieces
> Salted water to cover
> Approximately equal parts milk and half-and-half to cover potatoes by
>   1 to 2 inches (about 1½ to 2 cups each)
> 2 to 4 tablespoons butter (or to taste)
> ½ to 1 pound boneless, skinless walleye fillets (or other game fish fillets),
>   cut into ½-inch cubes
> Salt and freshly ground black pepper to taste

Bring potatoes, celery, and onions to a boil over high heat and cook until potatoes are tender. Drain and return to saucepan. Pour enough milk and half-and-half to cover potato mixture by 1 to 2 inches, depending on how hearty you want your soup. Add the butter and bring to a boil. Add walleye fillet cubes, cover pan, and remove from heat. Let stand covered for 10 minutes. Taste and add salt and pepper to taste. Makes about 1½ quarts.

Crappie Club Sandwiches with Garlic-Chive Mayonnaise

The sides of a slab crappie are just the right size for making sandwiches. For the best flavor scale the crappies before filleting. In panfish, as in most fish, some of the best flavor is in the skin.

> 1½ pounds boneless crappie or sunfish fillets, about 4 ounces for each sandwich
> Three-Step Breading (p. 210)
> 18 slices French, Italian, or other homemade-style bread approximately the size of the crappie fillets
> Lettuce leaves, as needed
> 12 thin slices of tomato
> 12 crisp bacon slices
> 1 recipe Garlic-Chive Mayonnaise (p. 61) or regular mayonnaise

Bread the crappie fillets with the Three-Step Breading using any of the variations as desired. *May be prepared up to several hours ahead and refrigerated.*

Prepare the Garlic-Chive Mayonnaise. Cover and refrigerate until needed.

Heat about ½ inch of oil in a large skillet set over medium-high heat until hot but not smoking. Fry the breaded crappies, in batches if necessary, until golden brown on both sides. Remove to paper towels to drain.

While the crappies are frying, toast the bread. For each sandwich, spread two of the three slices of toast liberally with the Garlic-Chive Mayonnaise. Place a lettuce leaf on one of the mayonnaise-covered slices and top with a fried crappie fillet or two, depending on how many you have. Place the plain slice of toast on top of the fish and top it with another lettuce leaf, a couple of tomato slices, and a couple of the crisp slices of bacon. Place the remaining mayonnaise-covered slice of toast on top, mayonnaise side down, of course, and secure the sandwich with two long toothpicks to hold it together. Slice the sandwich in two between the toothpicks. Makes 6 sandwiches.

Garlic-Chive Mayonnaise

> 1 cup mayonnaise
> 2 cloves garlic, peeled, crushed, and very finely chopped
> 2 tablespoons chopped chives
> Pinch of sugar
> Salt to taste
> Cayenne pepper to taste

Combine all ingredients in a bowl and whisk together until well combined. *May be made up to a week ahead and refrigerated covered.*

Buttermilk-Fried Panfish

Think that buttermilk is only for frying chicken? Think again. This is one of my favorite ways to fry up a mess of small fish fillets, such as sunfish, crappies, smallmouth bass, or perch, either in your kitchen or over a campfire. The buttermilk adds a tang to the breading that is delicious. But this is much too good to be limited to panfish. Follow this same breading procedure to make some very fine onion rings which, by the way, go well with a mess of buttermilk-fried fish.

> 2½ pounds boneless fish fillets
> 2 cups buttermilk
> ¼ teaspoon cayenne pepper
> Northwoods All-Purpose Breading Mix, as needed (p. 208)

Whisk together buttermilk and cayenne pepper. Place the fish fillets in a zipper-top bag or in a bowl and pour buttermilk mixture over the fish to cover. Marinate for 30 minutes to 1 hour in a cooler with ice or in the refrigerator.

Preheat oil to 360°F. Drain fish (a colander works well) or cut the corner off the zipper-top bag. Dredge in Northwoods All-Purpose Breading Mix, shake off the excess, and deep-fry until golden brown. Serves 6.

Raymie's Panfish and Shrimp Bake

My friend Ray Painter suggests serving this with some plain boiled potatoes, as the extra sauce makes an excellent gravy. (Who says you can't make gravy from fish?) He also recommends crusty French bread to mop up the sauce.

2½ tablespoons butter
2½ tablespoons flour
1 cup milk
Salt and red pepper (cayenne) to taste
4 ounces small cooked shrimp or larger cooked shrimp, coarsely chopped
1 medium onion, diced
1 tablespoon butter
2½ pounds boneless, skinless panfish or other game fish fillets
Salt and freshly ground black pepper to taste
Paprika
1 10½-ounce can cream of mushroom soup, undiluted (use low-fat version if desired)
3 to 4 ounces grated cheddar and/or American cheese

Preheat oven to 350°F. Make white sauce by melting 2½ tablespoons of butter in a heavy bottomed 1-quart saucepan over medium-low heat. Stir in 2½ tablespoons of flour and cook slowly for 1 minute without browning. Remove from heat and let cool a bit. Now whisk in 1 cup of cold milk all at once. Return the pan to medium heat and whisk constantly until sauce thickens and comes to a boil. The sauce will be quite thick. Stir in the shrimp. Remove from heat and season to taste with salt and red pepper. (Go light on the salt; the cream of mushroom soup is quite salty.) Cover shrimp sauce and keep warm while preparing onions and fish.

In a small skillet set over medium heat, sauté the onion in the butter until soft and transparent, but not brown. Scrape onions into the bottom of a shallow-sided baking dish large enough to hold the fish in a slightly overlapping layer.

Season fish fillets lightly with salt and pepper and dust lightly with paprika. Place the seasoned fillets in a slightly overlapping layer on top of the onions. Bake in preheated oven for 10 minutes to partially cook the fish.

Remove from oven and spread white sauce with shrimp evenly over the fish. Spoon the mushroom soup over the white sauce. Sprinkle the grated cheese over the top and bake for about 30 minutes or until the cheese is melted and the dish is bubbling around the sides. Remove from oven and let stand for 5 minutes before serving. Serves 6.

Try this with walleye or any boneless, skinless game fish fillets.

Foil-Baked Fish Fillets

Here is a tasty quick and easy way to cook fish in a foil package either in your oven or over a campfire. If you prepare a variety of the topping ingredients ahead of time, each person can build his or her own.

Preheat oven to 350°F or build a campfire well enough ahead of time to allow a good bed of coals to develop.

You will need one 6- to 8-ounce fillet per person. Lay each fillet on its own sheet of lightly greased foil and season lightly with salt and pepper or Ron Berg's Game-Fish Seasoning (p. 211).

Dot each fillet with 1 to 2 tablespoons of butter or use one of the flavorful compound butters listed on page 228. If you like, each fillet may also be drizzled with a tablespoon or so of dry white vermouth, dry white wine, fish stock/clam juice, cream, or a combination.

Now top with one or more of the items listed below. Add these with a light hand; we want to accent the flavor of the fish, not dominate it.

> Thinly sliced onions
> Thinly sliced fresh white, shiitake, or other wild mushrooms
> Thinly sliced green, red, or yellow peppers
> Crisp crumbled bacon
> Chopped fresh herbs—one herb such as basil, dill, chives, parsley, or
>   tarragon, or a combination, such as basil, chives, and parsley
> Peeled, seeded, and diced fresh tomatoes or drained, chopped, canned
>   tomatoes
> Blanched mixture of julienned carrots, leeks, celery, and onion

Now seal the foil with double folds. Bake in preheated oven for 12 to 18 minutes, depending on the size of the fillets, or bake on a grill over the coals of your campfire for 7 to 8 minutes on each side, more for thicker fillets. When turning foil packages, be careful not to puncture the foil or you will lose all the savory juices.

Cashew-Crusted Walleye

Cashews are the first nuts to disappear out of a can of mixed nuts. If you're a cashew fan, wait until you fry up your fish with this crunchy cashew breading. Other nuts (pecans are excellent) may be substituted if you like. Give this walleye recipe a try at your next fish fry.

> 4 ounces soda crackers (about ¾ cups pulverized) or cracker meal
> 1¼ cups salted cashews
> 1 tablespoon paprika
> ¾ teaspoon salt (or to taste)
> ⅛ teaspoon ground red pepper (cayenne)
> ¾ teaspoon ground white pepper (or to taste)
> All-purpose flour, as needed
> 2 large eggs, beaten
> Pinch of salt
> ½ cup liquid—water, white wine, milk, cream, evaporated milk, or beer
> 2½ pounds walleye fillets (not over ½ to ⅜ inch thick for best results)

To make the breading, combine the crackers, cashews, paprika, salt, and the red and white pepper in a food processor fitted with a metal blade. Process until the nuts are finely pulverized. Correct seasoning. Makes about 2 cups breading.

To bread the fish, shake them in a bag containing the all-purpose flour. Shake off the excess and dip each fillet into a mixture of the beaten eggs, a pinch of salt, and ½ cup of the chosen liquid. Then dredge or shake the fillets in the cashew breading. Place breaded fillets on a pan or plate and refrigerate until you are ready to fry them. *The fish may be breaded several hours in advance and refrigerated, or they may be frozen for up to a month.*

The breaded fillets may be panfried or deep-fried as desired. Serves 6.

Make the breading before you go and pack it in a double plastic bag. This recipe may be doubled. Try this breading with other fish such as panfish, northern pike, whitefish, catfish, perch, or bass.

Walleye Broiled in White Wine

This is the recipe I have always chosen for enjoying the first fresh walleye of the season. It is a simple pleasure and still one of my favorites. My second choice of fish for this recipe would be fresh whitefish fillets. As noted below, the fish may be broiled or baked with equal success.

> 2½ pounds walleye fillets
> 5 tablespoons butter, melted
> ¾ teaspoon fresh lemon juice
> ⅔ cup dry white vermouth or dry white wine
> Ron Berg's Game-Fish Seasoning (p. 211), lemon-pepper seasoning, or
>   salt and freshly ground black pepper to taste
> Paprika
> Chopped parsley for garnish (optional)
> Lemon wedges (optional)

Broiling Directions:

Preheat broiler. Lay walleye fillets on a shallow-sided sheet pan sprayed with nonstick cooking spray. Combine butter and lemon juice and brush the tops of the fillets liberally with the mixture. Season with choice of seasoning and sprinkle with paprika. Pour vermouth or white wine around the fillets.

Broil 2 to 4 inches from heat for 4 to 7 minutes or until fish is barely done. Remove carefully to heated plates or serving platter and drizzle the broiling juices over the fillets. Sprinkle with parsley and serve with lemon wedges. Serves 6.

Baking Directions:

Preheat oven to 450°F. Lay walleye fillets skin side down on a shallow-sided pan just large enough to hold the fillets in a single layer. Combine butter and lemon juice and brush the tops of the fillets liberally with the mixture. Season lightly with your choice of seasoning. Sprinkle with paprika. Pour vermouth or white wine *around* the fillets to avoid washing off seasonings. Bake in oven for 5 to 8 minutes or until fish just barely tests done. Remove fish to a heated serving platter and cover with foil. Pour pan juices into a skillet and reduce until lightly syrupy. Add any juices that have accumulated around the fish and drizzle reduced juices over the fillets. Sprinkle with parsley and serve with lemon wedges. Serves 6.

Broiled Walleye with Cream:

This is a wonderful variation of the recipe above. Prepare Walleye Broiled in White Wine, using either of the two methods above. When the fillets are done, remove them to a heated platter, cover, and keep warm while following the directions below.

Pour remaining pan juices into a stainless steel or enameled saucepan. Bring juices to a boil and add 1¼ cup heavy cream. Bring to a boil over high heat and reduce to a saucelike consistency. Add any juices that have collected around the fish to the sauce and season to taste with salt and white pepper. Spoon sauce around the broiled fillets and garnish with sprigs of parsley.

Baked Walleye Amandine

This is a baked version of a classic fish sauté with almonds. If you have individual gratin dishes that will accommodate a serving of walleye fillet, you can bake and serve the fish in the same dish. Setting the hot gratin dish on top of a napkin on a serving plate will keep the gratin dish from sliding around.

> 2½ pounds boneless, skinless walleye fillets
> ⅔ cup sliced almonds
> 6 tablespoons melted butter
> 2 to 2½ teaspoons fresh lemon juice (or to taste)
> 4 tablespoons finely chopped parsley
> Salt and freshly ground black pepper to taste

Preheat oven to 375°F. Butter a shallow baking dish or a large oval gratin dish that will just hold the fillets in a slightly overlapping layer. Sprinkle the almonds over the fish. Combine the melted butter and the lemon juice to taste and drizzle over the fish. Season lightly with salt and pepper and sprinkle the parsley over all. *May be made up to 2 hours ahead. Cover and refrigerate until ready to bake.*

Bake for 15 to 30 minutes, depending on the thickness of the fillets, or until fish is barely done. Serves 6.

Broiled Walleye with Parsley-Mustard Sauce

In this recipe the fish is broiled in white wine and the remaining wine and juices are transformed into a mellow mustard sauce flecked with parsley or chives.

> 2½ pounds walleye fillets (substitute boneless northern pike, bass, or other game fish fillets)
> Melted butter (3 to 4 tablespoons, or as needed)
> Salt and freshly ground black pepper
> Paprika
> ⅔ cup dry white vermouth or dry white wine
> 1¼ cups heavy cream
> 3 to 4 teaspoons Dijon mustard (or to taste)
> 2 tablespoons chopped parsley or fresh chives
> Salt and freshly ground black pepper to taste

Preheat oven to 450°F. Lay walleye fillets skin side down on a shallow-sided pan just large enough to hold the fillets in a single layer. Brush tops of fillets with melted butter and season lightly with salt and freshly ground black pepper. Sprinkle with paprika. Pour vermouth or white wine *around* the fillets to avoid washing off seasonings. Bake in oven for 5 to 8 minutes or until fish just barely tests done (fish will finish cooking while the sauce is being made). Remove fish from oven and pour the juices from the fish into a 10-inch skillet. Cover fish loosely with a piece of foil and set aside while you make the sauce.

Bring the reserved juices to a boil over high heat. Add the cream and reduce until saucelike. Whisk in the Dijon mustard to taste. Add the chopped parsley and season to taste with salt and pepper. Add any juices that have accumulated around the walleye to the sauce. Place the walleye on heated serving plates and spoon some of the sauce over each serving. Serves 6.

Lemon-Dijon-Butter Broiled Walleye Fillets

This easy recipe can be used with any game fish. If whole-grain Dijon is not available, use regular Dijon.

> 6 tablespoons butter, melted
> 1½ tablespoons whole-grain Dijon mustard
> 1 to 1½ tablespoons freshly squeezed lemon juice (or to taste)
> 2½ pounds walleye fillets
> Salt and freshly ground black pepper to taste
> Dry white wine
> Lemon twists and diagonally sliced green onion tops for garnish

Preheat oven to 450°F. In a small bowl, combine butter, Dijon mustard, and lemon juice. Lay the walleye fillets skin side down on a shallow-sided sheet pan. Brush the tops of the fillets with the butter mixture. Season the fish lightly with salt and pepper.

Bake for 5 to 7 minutes or until just barely done. Serve on heated plates. Garnish with lemon twists and sliced green onion tops. Serves 6.

Broiled Salmon or Trout Framstad

A guide often garners recipes from his clients. This fine (and easy) recipe is from Ken and Shirley Framstad. Another herb or mixture of herbs may be substituted for the dill weed.

> 2½ pounds salmon or trout fillets
> Melted butter, as needed
> Kosher salt and freshly ground black pepper to taste
> ¾ cup sour cream
> ¾ cup mayonnaise
> Dill weed to taste

Preheat the broiler if necessary. Place trout or salmon fillets skin side down on a broiler pan that has been sprayed with nonstick cooking spray. Brush the tops of the fillets with the melted butter and season lightly with salt and pepper.

Broil fillets 3 to 4 inches from the broiler until barely done. Whisk together the sour cream, mayonnaise, and dill weed. Spread mixture over the fish fillets and broil until bubbly. Transfer fish to heated serving plates. Serves 6.

Grilled Peppered Lake Trout

This simple recipe for grilled fish seasoned with black pepper and a soy sauce and butter baste will surely become one of your favorites, as it has mine. The fish may be cooked on a gas or charcoal grill, or over the coals of a campfire. My favorite way to grill these fish is over the coals of a hardwood fire, which imparts a fine smoky essence to the fish. Choice woods to use would be apple wood or other fruit woods, maple, alder, or hickory.

Leaving the skin on the fillets helps to keep the fish from breaking up on the grill. For a change of flavor, substitute Worcestershire sauce for the soy sauce.

> 2½ pounds lake trout or salmon fillets, skin on if possible, cut into 6 portions
> Coarsely ground black pepper to taste
> 9 tablespoons butter, melted
> 3 to 4 tablespoons soy sauce (or to taste)

Preheat gas grill or start charcoal or campfire well enough ahead of time to allow a good bed of hot coals to develop.

About 30 minutes before grilling, grind pepper coarsely over each portion of fish, pressing it into the flesh with the heel of your hand. Refrigerate for 30 minutes to allow the pepper to add flavor to the fish.

To grill the fish, combine the melted butter and soy sauce and brush the peppered side of the fish liberally with the mixture. Place fish on the grill with the peppered side down and baste the skin side with some of the baste. Grill for about 4 minutes, then turn fillets and brush with additional butter baste. Continue grilling, basting occasionally, for an additional 4 to 5 minutes or until fish is just barely cooked through, or, if using salmon fillets, cooked to desired doneness. Remove to heated plates and serve at once. Serves 6.

If you lack a pepper grinder or have one that can't be set to grind coarsely, the whole peppercorns may be coarsely cracked with the following restaurant method. Place a pile of peppercorns on your cutting board. Now take a 10-inch skillet, hold the handle in one hand, and put your other hand inside the skillet. Press down on the inside of the skillet with one hand, while using your other hand to pull the rounded bottom edge of the skillet across the peppercorns, tipping the pan onto its edge as you pull. You will hear them "popping" as they crack.

Fish Loaf

This is good comfort food and may be made with any leftover cooked fish or with canned fish. Try this with smoked fish or canned smoked fish.

> 2 cups boneless, cooked, and flaked fish (any kind) or 1 pint home-canned fish (p. 15) or 1-pound canned salmon, drained juices reserved
> ¼ cup butter, melted (optional)
> ¾ cup milk, or juices from canned fish plus enough milk to measure about ¾ cup
> ½ cup fresh white bread crumbs or coarsely crushed crackers
> 3 tablespoons finely chopped green pepper
> 1 celery stalk, minced
> 1 small onion, minced or grated
> 1 egg, beaten
> 1 tablespoon fresh lemon juice
> ½ teaspoon Worcestershire sauce
> 1 tablespoon chopped parsley
> ½ to 1 teaspoon kosher salt
> Freshly ground black pepper to taste
> ¼ cup shredded Swiss cheese (optional)
> Egg Sauce (optional, but recommended—recipe follows)

Preheat oven to 350°F. Mix salmon with the bread crumbs, the melted butter if you decide to use it, and the milk. If using crushed crackers, mix melted butter (if you decide to use it) with fish juices and milk and pour over crackers. Mix well and let stand for 5 minutes, then mix into fish in place of the bread crumbs and milk.

Add the beaten egg and stir into fish mixture. Stir in remaining ingredients and combine well. Spoon into a greased 1-quart loaf pan or casserole dish. Bake uncovered until just firm, approximately 25 to 35 minutes. The exact time will vary depending on the width and depth of the baking pan. Cool on cake rack for 5 minutes, then invert onto serving platter. Serve with Egg Sauce, if desired. Serves 4.

Egg Sauce

> 1 cup medium white sauce (see recipe in note below)
> 1 to 2 hard-boiled eggs, finely chopped
> 1½-inch strand of anchovy paste from tube (optional—see note below)
> ¼ teaspoon dry mustard
> ½ teaspoon Dijon mustard (or to taste)
> Salt and white pepper to taste

Combine all ingredients and heat to a simmer. Thin with milk if too thick.

To make a cup of medium white sauce, melt 2 tablespoons of butter in a heavy bottomed 1-quart saucepan over medium-low heat. Stir in 2 tablespoons of flour and cook for 1 minute without browning. Remove from heat and let cool a bit. Now whisk in 1 cup of cold milk all at once. Return the pan to medium heat and whisk constantly until sauce thickens and comes to a boil. Remove from heat and season to taste with salt and white pepper. If sauce becomes too thick, whisk in additional milk.

Anchovy paste is sold in squeeze tubes and is available in supermarkets.

Things Too Fierce to Mention

Some years ago, a guitar-playing friend used to sing a silly song called "A Horse Named Bill" sung to the tune of "Dixie." Several of the verses concerned a whale who lived in Frisco Bay. One of the verses went like this:

> She loves to laugh and when she smiles
> You just see teeth for miles and miles.
> And tonsils . . . and spareribs. . . .
> And things too fierce to mention.

Our forebears referred to innards as "livers and lights." One usually doesn't think of fish in terms of internal goodies, but nevertheless some fishermen love these delicious extras.

Sautéed Northern Pike Livers

If this recipe sounds like a perverse joke, let me assure you it is not. Dave Roberts, one-time fishing guide for the old End of the Trail Lodge on Saganaga Lake during the early 1960s, introduced me to these tasty tidbits. Dave always seemed to lack the walleye guide's usual aversion to northern pike, that bony-fleshed predator that often relieves the walleye fisherman of his terminal tackle with its sharp teeth. In fact, Dave actually thrives on them during his stays at his remote cabin. This is due, perhaps, not only to the mile-and-a-half hike from the nearest road (which sharpens the appetite), but to the absence of any other fish in waters adjacent to his place. This is his recipe and I have to admit that these pike livers are delicious, tasting somewhat like chicken livers.

If you catch a northern or two and plan a meal from them, the sautéed livers, cut into pieces and served with toothpicks, make a good appetizer to munch on while the fish is being cooked. They could also be served on a bed of wild rice for a unique first course. Lake trout, stream trout, and walleye livers are also superb and can be substituted for the northern livers in this recipe.

> Northern pike (or other game fish) livers, any amount
> Salt and freshly ground black pepper
> Flour, as needed
> Butter and vegetable oil (2 parts butter to 1 part vegetable oil)

Cut the liver into 1-inch chunks and season lightly with salt and pepper. Dredge in flour and shake off the excess. Heat the butter and vegetable oil in a skillet set over medium-high heat and sauté the livers until they are just light pink in the center. Do not overcook.

Sautéed Fish Roe

Since lake trout are fall spawners, female trout caught in the summer often contain roe or eggs. In winter and early spring, sunfish and crappies also contain eggs.

To use the roe, the eggs must be removed from the fish with its sac intact. You will find two such sacs in each female fish. Roe is very perishable, so it either must be used at once or kept as cold as possible without freezing it. Another caution is not to overcook the roe, which will make it tough.

All that being said and done, what does one do with roe? I have read recipes describing the making of your own caviar from it, but the only way I have prepared it is by parboiling and sautéing. Follow the recipe below or use your favorite fish breading.

Rinse the roe sacs in cold water and gently pat them dry with paper towels. Parboil the roe sacs by dropping them into boiling water to which salt and lemon juice have been added. Immediately reduce the heat to very low and gently simmer the roe until the sacs start to turn opaque. Gently remove the sacs with a slotted spoon and drop into very cold water. When cold, drain the roe and divide the sacs into large pieces. The smaller egg sacs of panfish do not need to be divided.

Dip the pieces of roe into an egg beaten with 3 tablespoons of cream and dredge in a flour mixture consisting of 1 cup flour seasoned with 1 teaspoon salt, ¼ teaspoon black pepper, and 2 teaspoons paprika. Fry in a mixture of butter and oil (2 parts butter to 1 part oil) until brown and crisp, turning only once. Serve on buttered toast with lemon butter drizzled over the top.

Fish Cheeks Prepared Scampi Style

Although fish cheeks don't really qualify as innards, they are included here for lack of a better place to present these delicious morsels. The cheeks are referred to by some as the filet mignon of the fish. The cheeks of both walleye and lake trout are superb eating. Use the tip of the fillet knife to cut a semicircle around the soft cushion of meat directly behind the eye. When you have freed the cheek meat from the head of the fish, use your thumb to completely remove the cheek, peeling it off of the skin still attached to the head.

Eat them as you get them or freeze them in a bag until you get enough for this special recipe. Serve this with crusty French bread for sopping up the garlicky juices.

> 4 ounces walleye or lake trout cheeks
> Salt and freshly ground black pepper
> 3 tablespoons butter
> 1 clove garlic, minced
> 1 tablespoon dry white vermouth or dry white wine
> 2 to 3 tablespoons freshly grated Parmesan cheese
> 1 teaspoon chopped fresh parsley

Melt the butter in a skillet set over medium heat. When sizzling, add the garlic and stir for 15 seconds without browning the garlic. Add the vermouth or wine and the fish cheeks and sauté, tossing and turning them until they turn white and are just barely cooked through. Do not overcook or the cheeks will become chewy. Use a rubber spatula to scrape the cheeks and garlic butter into a heated serving dish. Top with Parmesan cheese and a sprinkling of parsley. Serves 2 as an appetizer.

Chapter 4

Appetizers,
Soups,
and
First Courses

J ust like a good bottle of wine, exciting beginnings add considerably to the enjoyment of any meal. Many of the recipes included here may be prepared ahead of time, so they can be quickly heated when you are ready to serve.

Additional appetizers and soups are found elsewhere in this book. Smoked fish (p. 165) makes a wonderful appetizer when served with Chive-Horseradish Sauce (p. 223), crackers, and some thinly sliced sweet onions.

Use the beer batter recipe (p. 209) to make beer-batter-fried fish fingers and serve them with any of the tartar sauces (p. 222, 223), the Cocktail Sauce (p. 224), the Tomato-Basil Remoulade (p. 224), or the Curry-Dijon Mayonnaise (p. 225). Use the beer batter to deep-fry mushrooms, broccoli, cauliflower, or other vegetables for tasty, golden, crisp appetizer bites to serve along with the fish or by themselves.

Other fine beginnings are the traditional Finnish fish soup, Mojakka (p. 59), and two soups from the smoker, Creamy Smoke-Roasted Onion Soup with Parmesan Cheese (p. 174), and Cream of Smoked Wild Forest Mushroom Soup (p. 176).

Beer Corn Batter–Fried Walleye Fingers with Green Chile Aioli and Cucumber-Tomato Relish

This wonderful crunchy walleye appetizer with spicy Southwestern flavors has been a perennial favorite in the dining room at Gunflint Lodge since it first appeared on the menu. A classic French aioli (pronounced aye-OH-lee) is a garlic-flavored mayonnaise. Green chiles and fresh lime juice add an adventurous élan to this aioli. The spicy sweet-sour relish is a perfect foil to the crisp walleye and the creamy aioli.

Green Chile Aioli

1 cup mayonnaise
1 teaspoon minced garlic
1 roasted poblano chile, peeled, seeded, and cut into 1–inch pieces
½ to 1 roasted jalapeño pepper, peeled and seeded (optional)
1 tablespoon fresh lime juice (or to taste)
Salt and freshly ground black pepper to taste

Cucumber-Tomato Relish

Start out with less of those ingredients calling for varying amounts, then add more to taste. To cut the heat of the jalapeño even more, remove the ribs along with the seeds.

1 cucumber, seeded and cut into ¼- or ⅜-inch dice
1 tomato, seeded and cut into ¼- or ⅜-inch dice
3 tablespoons onions, minced
½ to 1 jalapeño pepper, seeded and finely diced
2 to 3 tablespoons rice vinegar (or to taste)
¼ to ½ teaspoon salt (or to taste)
2 to 3 tablespoons sugar (or to taste)

Southwestern Beer Corn Batter

This is very similar to the Beer Corn Batter recipe on page 209. Here I have substituted red chile powder made from New Mexico red chiles for the paprika. If you don't have the red chile powder, simply omit it.

1 cup flour
2 teaspoons salt
1 teaspoon freshly ground black pepper

½ teaspoon ground red chile powder (*molido*—optional)

½ cup yellow cornmeal

1 teaspoon dry mustard

⅛ teaspoon cayenne pepper

Beer, as needed

1½ pounds walleye fillets, cut into finger-sized pieces

Flour, as needed

To make the aioli, place mayonnaise, garlic, poblano chile, jalapeño, and lime juice in a food processor and process with a metal blade until pureed. Season to taste with salt and pepper. Strain through a sieve and put into a plastic squeeze bottle. Refrigerate until needed. *May be made up to 2 weeks ahead and stored in the refrigerator.*

To make the relish, combine diced cucumber, tomatoes, onions, and jalapeño with rice vinegar, salt, and sugar to taste. *May be made several hours ahead and refrigerated until needed.*

To make the beer corn batter, combine dry ingredients and whisk in enough beer to make the batter as thick as paint.

To fry the fish, heat oil in a deep-fat fryer or deep pan to 360°F. Place about a cup of flour in a bag or shallow pan, such as a pie tin. Shake or dredge walleye fingers in the flour. Remove the pieces one at a time from the flour; shake off excess flour. Dip flour-coated walleye in the batter one at a time and drop gently into the hot fat, being careful not to crowd the fryer. Remove with a slotted spoon when golden brown and crisp; drain on paper towels. Serve immediately.

Use the squeeze bottle of aioli to make a zig-zag or spiral design on a large round plate. Place a mound of drained relish in center of plate. Lay fried walleye fingers on the aioli, radiating out from the relish in a spoke fashion. Top with some sliced green onion tops if desired for garnish. Serve extra aioli on the side, if desired. Makes 6 appetizer or first-course servings.

Poblano chiles vary greatly in heat, ranging from mild to wild. Add the optional jalapeño to make the aioli hotter.

Beer corn batter will thicken shortly after the beer is whisked in. Add additional beer as needed to maintain correct consistency.

Wilderness Walleye and Shrimp Croquettes with Horseradish Tartar Sauce and Northwoods Dressed Greens

These crisp, golden brown walleye and shrimp patties are flavored with curry, Dijon mustard, and other savory seasonings. I like to serve them as a first course with Horseradish Tartar Sauce (p. 223) and some fresh greens tossed with dried cranberries and a quintessential northwoods vinaigrette made with maple syrup (recipe below).

> 13½ to 14 ounces boneless, skinless walleye fillets
> 6 ounces shrimp, peeled and deveined
> 1 large egg, lightly beaten
> 1 tablespoon mayonnaise
> 2 tablespoons Dijon mustard (or to taste)
> 1 to 1½ teaspoons freshly ground black pepper (or to taste)
> ½ teaspoon curry powder
> 3 to 4 drops hot pepper sauce
> 1 teaspoon Worcestershire sauce
> ¼ teaspoon cayenne pepper
> ¾ teaspoon celery salt
> ½ teaspoon salt (more to taste)
> 3 to 6 tablespoons dry bread crumbs, as needed for consistency
> 1 to 2 cups additional dry bread crumbs for breading

Using a food processor with a metal blade, pulse to coarsely chop the walleye and shrimp. Transfer to a large bowl. In a medium-sized bowl, whisk together the egg with the remaining ingredients except for the bread crumbs. Stir egg mixture into walleye and shrimp and combine thoroughly. Stir in enough dry bread crumbs to hold mixture together. Fry up a small patty and taste for seasoning.

Form into patties using approximately 2 heaping tablespoons per patty and dredge in dry bread crumbs. (A #50 scoop [1 ounce] commonly used for cookies makes perfect-sized patties. Simply scoop and drop into dry bread crumbs, then use hands to form into patties.) Place finished patties on a sheet pan and refrigerate for one hour. *May be frozen on the sheet pan after cooling and removed to plastic freezer bags and sealed tightly after they are frozen. The frozen patties may be fried as needed directly from the freezer.* Makes about 30 1½-inch patties.

Northwoods Dressed Greens

> Julienned mixed greens or julienned fresh spinach, as needed
> Dried cranberries (craisins), as needed

Maple Vinaigrette

This recipe may be doubled or more as desired.

> 1 tablespoon red wine vinegar
> 1 teaspoon minced red onion
> ½ teaspoon Dijon mustard (or to taste)
> 3 tablespoons olive oil
> 1 tablespoon pure maple syrup (or to taste)
> Salt and freshly ground black pepper to taste

To make the vinaigrette, whisk together the red wine vinegar, minced red onion, and Dijon mustard. Slowly whisk in the olive oil. Whisk in the maple syrup and season to taste with salt and freshly ground black pepper. *May be made several days ahead and refrigerated until needed. Let warm for a short time at room temperature before using.*

To serve as a first course, fry one breaded patty per person in a heavy bottomed skillet set over medium heat with ⅛ inch vegetable oil in bottom until golden brown on both sides. Patties may also be deep-fried at 350°F. Drain on paper towels.

Spoon a pool of Horseradish Tartar Sauce in the middle of each plate. Toss the greens with dried cranberries and Maple Vinaigrette to taste and place some of the dressed greens around one side of the tartar sauce. On the other side place a hot deep-fried croquette with one edge overlapping the tartar sauce.

The croquettes may also be served as an appetizer along with Horseradish Tartar Sauce to dip them in.

Puttin' on the Ritz: Deep-Fried Walleye Nuggets and Morel Mushrooms

This is my old friend Raymie Painter's recipe. If his fishing and foraging have been successful, Raymie enjoys this Minnesota specialty every spring.

1 cup flour, seasoned to taste with salt and pepper
3 eggs, well beaten
1 cup heavy cream
1 pound walleye fillets, cut into 1-inch pieces
2 dozen fresh morel mushrooms, cut in half if large
Finely crushed Ritz® crackers as needed

Place the flour in a flat shallow container, such as a pie tin, and the cracker crumbs in another. In a small bowl whisk together the eggs and cream. Flour the walleye and morel pieces and shake off the excess. Dip the floured pieces into the egg-cream mixture, then bread them with the cracker crumbs. Place the breaded fish and mushrooms in a single layer on a sheet pan and refrigerate for at least 30 minutes to allow the breading to firm up. Deep-fry the walleye pieces and the mushrooms until golden brown and crisp. Drain on paper towels and serve hot. Serves 4 to 6 as an appetizer.

Northwoods Game Fish Chowder

Common to fishing camps all over the north, this hearty fish chowder is made from the trimmings of the day's catch. Any fish, including the more oily varieties such as salmon and lake trout, may be used to make this hearty chowder.

> 3 tablespoons butter
> 2 to 3 cups chopped onions
> 2 to 3 cups ½-inch diced potatoes
> 1 quart White Wine Fish Stock (p. 216) or ¼ cup dry white wine plus
>   4 7-ounce bottles clam juice
> 1 cup heavy cream or 1 8-ounce can evaporated milk
> ½ pound game fish fillets, cut into cubes (use more as desired)
> Salt and freshly ground black pepper to taste
> Hot pepper sauce to taste
> Oyster crackers

In medium stockpot set over low heat, cook onions in butter until transparent. Add potatoes and fish stock or wine and clam juice. Increase heat to medium-high and bring to a boil. Reduce heat; simmer until potatoes are tender. Add cream or evaporated milk and fish. Simmer for 10 minutes or until fish is cooked. Season to taste with salt, pepper, and hot pepper sauce. Serve with oyster crackers. Serves 4 to 6.

Malaysian Steamboat with Walleye and Shrimp

This is my northwoods version of a traditional Malaysian soup recipe I learned from Peter Bung, a native of Malaysia who worked at Gunflint Lodge one summer. This soup lends itself to endless variations. Besides fish and shrimp, small pieces of pork, chicken, beef, or vegetables, either by themselves or in combination, may also be cooked and served in the finished broth. Note that the broth itself is not highly flavored. The addition of the spicy Chile–Soy Sauce Condiment is what really makes this soup shine.

Steamboat Stock

2 14½-ounce cans low-sodium chicken broth
2 14½-ounce cans water
Shrimp shells from 6 to 8 ounces of shrimp
1 small onion, chopped fine
2 cloves garlic, peeled and halved
4 dime-sized slices fresh ginger

Chile–Soy Sauce Condiment

⅓ cup soy sauce
1 to 2 teaspoons chile paste with garlic (more to taste)
Diagonal sliced green onions for garnish

2 teaspoons Oriental sesame oil (more to taste)
Salt to taste
8 ounces boneless, skinless walleye or other game fish, cut into ¾-inch cubes
6 ounces small, whole, raw shrimp or large shrimp cut into ½-inch pieces
2 to 3 cups iceberg or romaine lettuce, cut or torn as for salad
About ¼ pound of dry pasta, such as angel hair or spaghetti, cooked and
    cut into 2-inch lengths or 1½ cups of cooked rice

To make the Steamboat Stock, combine chicken broth, water, shrimp shells, onion, garlic, and ginger in a 1½- or 2-quart saucepan. Bring to a boil over high heat, then reduce heat to low and simmer gently for 30 minutes. While stock is simmering, make the Chile–Soy Sauce Condiment by mixing the chile paste to taste with soy sauce.

Strain the stock, add the sesame oil, and lightly season to taste with salt, as the Chile–Soy Sauce Condiment added later is quite salty. *May be made up to 3 days ahead and refrigerated. The stock may be frozen for longer storage of up to 6 months.* Add diced walleye and the shrimp to the stock and simmer for 5 minutes over medium heat. Just before serving, add the lettuce leaves to the soup and bring to a simmer. Ladle hot soup over pasta or rice in bowls. Sprinkle with the green onions and pass the Chile–Soy Sauce Condiment. Serves 6.

Chile paste with garlic is a fiery condiment sold in Asian grocery stores and in the specialty food sections of many supermarkets. Use it sparingly as it is very hot. It is sometimes labeled chile sauce with garlic. If you can't stand any heat, it can be omitted and soy sauce alone can be added to the soup to taste.

For additional flavor, chicken bones or pork bones may also be added with the shrimp shells. Simmer for an additional 1½ hours to extract all the flavor from the bones.

Walleye and Pistachio Nut Sausage

Everybody likes these elegant sausages. They have been on the appetizer menu for several years in the dining room at Gunflint Lodge. For an extra special presentation, serve these with Ron's Beurre Blanc Sauce (p. 234).

4 walleye fillets, 6 to 8 ounces each, skinned and cut into 1-inch chunks
12 ounces small shrimp
4 ounces bay scallops
6 egg whites
2 tablespoons cognac or brandy
⅜ teaspoon cayenne
4 to 6 teaspoons fresh lemon juice (1 small lemon)
1½ teaspoons Walleye Sausage Seasoning (recipe follows)
1 to 1½ cups heavy cream, as needed
12 ounces imitation crab, coarsely chopped
2 cups coarsely chopped shrimp
4 ounces pistachio nuts, shelled and chopped
½ cup chopped fresh parsley
Salt to taste
Fresh white bread crumbs, as needed for proper consistency
Sausage casings

In a food processor with a metal blade, puree walleye, shrimp, and scallops. Add egg whites, cognac or brandy, cayenne, lemon juice, and 1½ teaspoons of the seasoning mix. Process for 30 seconds. With machine running, slowly pour in enough cream to produce a mixture that will hold its shape in a spoon. Scrape into a large bowl and refrigerate for at least 15 minutes.

In the same processor bowl, add crab and shrimp. Pulse to chop coarsely. Fold seafood into chilled sausage mixture. Add the chopped pistachios and the chopped parsley. If mixture is too soft, add fresh white bread crumbs as needed for proper consistency; mix well. In a small skillet, sauté small amount to taste for seasoning. Add salt to taste if needed. Refrigerate for 1 hour.

Stuff sausage mixture into prepared sausage casings; tie into

4-inch links. Place the sausages into barely simmering water and cook gently until the internal temperature reaches 165°F when checked with an instant-read thermometer. Place the sausages in ice water until cold. Wrap individually in plastic wrap and freeze in bags. Makes about 20 to 24 4-inch sausage links.

▶━━━ If you do not have casings or prefer not to use them, you may form the sausage into small patties. Use a #50 (1 ounce) scoop (the popular size for cookies) or a spoon to measure out 2 table-spoons of the sausage mixture and place in a greased preheated skillet or griddle set over medium heat (or in an electric griddle with the temperature set at 350°F). Cook until bottoms are barely set, then flip over and flatten each one with the spatula to make round sausage patties about 1½ inches in diameter. Partially cook-ing the sausages on one side prevents them from sticking to the spatula when being flattened. When brown, flip over onto partially cooked side and cook until cooked through. Do not overcook or the sausages will be dry. Use the cooked patties within 3 days or freeze individually on a cookie sheet. When frozen, place patties in a heavy-duty plastic bag and seal tightly.

To serve the patties, thaw, if frozen, and heat until hot in a 400°F oven. *Both the links and the patties may be frozen for up to 6 months.*

Walleye Sausage Seasoning

Makes enough for several recipes.

> 2 tablespoons ground white pepper
> 2¼ teaspoons ground nutmeg
> 1 tablespoon ground coriander
> ¾ teaspoon ground cloves
> 1½ teaspoons onion powder
> 5 tablespoons salt

Combine all ingredients and mix well.

Mediterranean Fish Soup with Tomatoes and Fresh Basil

This fish soup, replete with good things from the garden, would be just the thing to enjoy on the deck on a lazy summer evening with crickets chirping in the background. Pour a glass of sauvignon blanc and savor this soup along with a loaf of crusty French bread.

2 tablespoons olive oil
2 cloves garlic, minced
1 medium onion, chopped
¼ teaspoon crushed red pepper flakes (or to taste)
½ cup dry white vermouth or dry white wine
2 cups peeled, seeded, and diced Roma or other firm ripe tomatoes
    (about 4 to 6)
2½ cups White Wine Fish Stock (p. 216) or bottled clam juice
1 pound boneless skinless game fish fillets, one or more kinds, cubed
½ cup chopped fresh basil
Salt and freshly ground black pepper to taste
Hot pepper sauce to taste (optional)

In a large saucepan set over low heat, sauté the garlic, onion, and red pepper flakes in the olive oil until the onions are soft and transparent. Add the dry white vermouth and tomatoes, and increase heat to high. Bring to a boil and reduce by one half. Reduce heat to medium-low and add the fish stock or clam juice. Simmer slowly for 10 minutes. Add the cubed fish and simmer for an additional 10 minutes. Stir in the chopped basil and season to taste with salt, pepper, and hot pepper sauce to taste.

Lake Trout and Wild Rice Sausage with Morel Mushroom Sauce

These sausages have a wonderful meaty flavor. They make an elegant first course when served with a wild mushroom sauce, which goes extremely well with the meaty taste of these sausages. This sauce is especially delicious made with fresh morel mushrooms, but other wild mushrooms are nearly as delicious and easier to find. Morels are now being farm raised and while not as flavorful as their wild cousins, they are available in some supermarket produce sections all year round.

These sausages are also delicious smoked. Instead of cooking them in water after stuffing in casings, place sausage links in a smoker and hot smoke (250°F degrees) until cooked through, or finish cooking in a 250°F oven after desired smoke flavor and color is reached. The smoked sausages may be served hot or sliced cold and eaten on crackers with mayonnaise mixed with horseradish and chives to taste.

2 tablespoons butter
1 medium onion, finely diced
1 small clove garlic, finely minced
6 ounces crabmeat or surimi (imitation crab)
1½ pounds skinless, boneless lake trout fillets, cut into chunks
1 large egg
1 egg white
2 teaspoons cognac or brandy
1 to 1½ cups heavy cream
1 tablespoon tomato paste
2 tablespoons Lake Trout and Wild Rice Sausage Seasoning Mix
    (recipe follows)
1 teaspoon fresh lemon juice (or to taste)
¼ cup chopped parsley
1 cup cooked wild rice (about ⅓ cup uncooked)
Dry bread crumbs, as needed to firm up consistency
Salt to taste

Sauté the onion and garlic in the butter over low heat until the onion is transparent. Set aside to cool. In a food processor with a metal blade, pulse the crabmeat to coarsely chop. Scrape into a bowl and refrigerate until needed. In the same food-processor bowl, puree the lake trout. Add the egg, the egg white, cognac or brandy, and tomato paste. With the machine running, slowly pour in the cream until the mixture is light and fluffy. Scrape into a large bowl and add the sautéed onions and garlic, reserved crabmeat, tomato paste, 2 tablespoons of the seasoning mix, lemon juice, parsley, and cooked wild rice. Mix well, adding dry white bread crumbs as needed. Fry up a small portion and taste for seasoning, adding additional salt and lemon juice to taste.

At this point the sausage mixture may be either stuffed into casings or formed into patties and fried. Both may be frozen for up to 6 months.

To make patties, use a #50 (1 ounce) scoop (the popular size for cookies) or a spoon to measure out 2 tablespoons of the sausage mixture and place in a greased preheated skillet or griddle set over medium heat (or an electric griddle with the temperature set at 350°F). Cook until bottoms are barely set, then flip over and flatten each one with the spatula to make round sausage patties about 1½ inches in diameter. Partially cooking the sausages on one side prevents them from sticking to the spatula when being flattened. When brown, flip over onto partially cooked side and cook until cooked through. Do not overcook or the sausages will be dry. Cool and refrigerate or freeze. Makes about 10 4-inch sausage links, or 35 to 40 sausage patties.

Lake Trout and Wild Rice Sausage Seasoning Mix

2 teaspoons ground white pepper
¾ teaspoon nutmeg
1 teaspoon ground coriander
¼ teaspoon ground cloves
½ teaspoon onion powder
2½ teaspoons paprika
5 teaspoons salt

Combine all ingredients and mix well. Makes about ¼ cup.

Wild Mushroom Sauce

> 2 tablespoons butter
> ¼ teaspoon minced garlic
> 3 tablespoons minced onions
> 1½ cups halved fresh morel mushrooms or other sliced wild mushrooms,
>   such as shiitakes, oyster, chanterelle, or a mixture
> ¼ cup dry white vermouth or dry white wine
> 1¼ cups heavy cream
> Kosher salt and freshly ground black pepper to taste

To make the Wild Mushroom Sauce, melt the butter in a skillet set over medium-low heat and sauté the garlic for 30 seconds or so without browning. Add the onions and cook until transparent. Add the wild mushrooms and continue cooking until the mushrooms soften and give up their juices. Add the wine and increase heat to medium-high. Bring to a boil and reduce by one half. Add the heavy cream and reduce to a saucelike consistency. Season to taste with salt and pepper. *May be made up to 3 days ahead and refrigerated, or frozen for up to 6 months.* Makes about 1½ cups sauce.

To serve the patties, place on a shallow-sided sheet pan and heat until hot in a preheated 400°F oven. Serve one or two of the patties per person as a first course with 2 to 3 tablespoons of the Wild Mushroom Sauce.

To stuff into casings: Refrigerate sausage mixture for 1 hour before stuffing casings. Stuff into prepared sausage casings and divide into 4-inch links by twisting or tying with short lengths of string. Place the sausages in barely simmering water and cook gently until the internal temperature reaches 165°F when checked with an instant-read thermometer. Immediately place the sausages in ice water and cool completely. Refrigerate for up to 3 days or wrap and freeze for up to 6 months.

To serve the links, sauté them in butter until browned and heated through. Slice diagonally and fan out. Serve 1 link per person as a first course with 2 to 3 tablespoons of the Wild Mushroom Sauce.

Walleye en Croute

Imagine a walleye fillet baked in a crisp, golden brown, puff pastry crust! Frozen puff pastry makes this restaurant specialty possible for the home cook. For an elegant first course, serve with a Chive Hollandaise Sauce (p. 233) and steamed broccoli spears or fresh asparagus.

> 1 package frozen puff pastry, thawed according to package directions
> 4 tablespoons butter, melted
> 4 tablespoons dry white vermouth or dry white wine
> 12 ounces boneless skinless walleye fillets
> Salt and freshly ground black pepper
> 2 tablespoons chopped parsley
> 1 large egg, beaten
> 2 tablespoons milk

On a lightly floured surface, roll out one of the puff pastry sheets with a rolling pin to make it large enough to cut out 2 circles approximately 8 inches in diameter. Repeat with the second sheet of puff pastry, cutting 2 more circles.

Cut the walleye into 3-ounce portions. If necessary, you can put together small pieces to equal about 3 ounces. Combine the melted butter and vermouth or white wine. Lay out the circles on a lightly floured board. Brush the centers of the circles with the butter-wine mixture, leaving a 1-inch border around the edges. Place the walleye portions on the lower half of each circle and season lightly with salt and pepper and sprinkle with some of the parsley.

Whisk the egg into the remaining butter-wine mixture and brush the edges of the circles. Fold over the tops of the circles and seal by making overlapping folds or by pressing with the tines of a fork.

Use a spatula to place the puff pastry packages on an ungreased baking pan. Whisk the milk into the remaining egg and butter mixture to make a wash to glaze the pastries with. Brush the tops of the pastries with this mixture, being careful not to let any of the glaze run off the edges. This might "pin" the pastry to the pan and prevent puffing.

Roll out some of the remaining puff pastry scraps to make decorations such as cutouts or braids. Dip the decorations into the egg wash and place on top of the pastries. There is no need to make air vents in the pastry. *Recipe may be made several hours ahead to this point and refrigerated uncovered.*

Preheat oven to 350°F. Bake the puff pastry packages for 40 to 45 minutes or until puffed and golden brown. Makes 4 first-course servings.

Lake Superior Salmon Cakes

Serve these savory cakes as an elegant first course with either a tangy Tomato-Basil Remoulade sauce (p. 224) or an earthy Curry-Dijon Mayonnaise (p. 225). Or form into larger patties and serve on a soft hamburger bun topped with crisp lettuce and either of the two sauces.

> 1 pound boneless salmon cut into large cubes
> 2 tablespoons chopped shallots
> 1 large egg, beaten
> ½ cup fresh white bread crumbs, or more as needed for consistency
> 1 teaspoon soy sauce
> 1 tablespoon Dijon mustard
> ¾ to 1 teaspoon kosher salt (or to taste)
> Freshly ground black pepper to taste

In a food processor fitted with a metal blade, coarsely chop the salmon. Scrape salmon into a bowl and combine with the remaining ingredients, mixing well (mixture will be sticky). Fry up a small patty to taste for seasoning. Shape with floured hands into 6 burgers or 12 appetizer cakes. Panfry patties in butter in a skillet over medium heat until done about medium well. Remove to paper towels to drain. Makes 6 sandwiches or 6 large or 12 small first-course servings.

To make the fresh bread crumbs, use a food processor fitted with a metal blade. Simply remove crusts from white bread, cut into cubes, and pulse in the processor.

Chapter 5

Elegant Entrées

As a chef I have always been fascinated by the great versatility of fish in the kitchen. Most people's favorite way to eat fish, of course, is panfried or deep-fried. To be sure, the moist, sweet succulence of a freshly caught fish fillet encased in a thin, crisp, golden brown crust is indeed food for the gods, but to limit the fish we eat to frying alone is to deny our palate some incredibly fine eating. And life is just too short for that.

In this chapter you will find new and exciting possibilities for preparing the fish you catch (or purchase). Don't let that word "elegant" in the chapter title scare you. Elegant doesn't necessarily mean difficult. In fact many of the recipes in this chapter are extraordinarily easy to prepare. Some require multiple steps, which may make them appear more difficult than they really are.

Actually, what we may think of as very ordinary foods can be made to look quite elegant with the right presentation. We feast first with our eyes, therefore we should put as much effort into making our food look nice as we do into making it taste good.

Becoming an accomplished cook means acquiring various skills. It is a lifelong learning process, as well as a gradual one. How do we learn? Some go to culinary schools or take cooking classes. Others learn primarily from cookbooks, the best of which are as good a source of knowledge as they are of recipes. And today there is an entire television network devoted to food and cooking. Finally there is the Internet, which provides an endless source of cooking information and recipes.

Walleye with Green Chile Stuffing

This Southwestern-style stuffing can be made as spicy as you want by adjusting the amount of jalapeños. You may omit them for a milder stuffing. Be forewarned: fresh poblano chiles can vary from quite mild to very hot. Canned chopped green chiles are very mild.

Green Chile Stuffing

¼ cup butter
½ teaspoon minced garlic
¼ cup finely chopped onions
½ to 1 jalapeño pepper, seeds removed and finely chopped (optional)
1 poblano chile, roasted, peeled, seeded, and finely diced
   or 1 (4½-ounce) can chopped green chiles
1 teaspoon ground cumin (or to taste)
2 tablespoons chopped flat leaf (Italian) parsley
1 tablespoon chopped green onion tops
1 quart fresh white bread crumbs
Heavy cream as needed to moisten
2 ounces (½ cup) shredded Monterey Jack cheese, coarsely chopped
Salt and freshly ground black pepper
Drops of fresh lime juice to taste

Tomato Compote

1 firm ripe tomato, seeded and diced
1 tablespoon minced red or yellow onion
1 teaspoon red wine vinegar
1 teaspoon chopped flat leaf parsley
Salt and fresh ground black pepper to taste
A pinch or two of sugar to taste

2½ pounds boneless, skinless walleye or other game fish fillets or whole
   prepared fish
4 to 5 ounces (1 to 1¼ cups) additional shredded Monterey Jack cheese
   for topping (optional)

Make Green Chile Stuffing: In a 10-inch skillet set over low heat, melt butter and add garlic, onions, and the jalapeño if you decide to use it. Cover pan and sweat onion mixture until onions are translucent. Stir in the poblano chiles or the canned green chiles and the ground cumin. Add the parsley, green onion tops, and the bread crumbs and toss to combine. Add cream to moisten. Stir in the chopped Monterey Jack cheese. Season to taste with salt and pepper and drops of fresh lime juice. *May be made up to 3 days ahead and refrigerated.*

Make Tomato Compote by combining all ingredients. *For best results make just before serving.*

Stuff and bake fish using one of the methods suggested for fillets or whole fish on page 200. If using the Two-Fillet Method of stuffing, top the exposed stuffing with additional Monterey Jack cheese before baking if desired.

Serve on heated plates with the Tomato Compote sprinkled over and around fish. For a superelegant presentation, drizzle with one or more of the Desert Paint Sauces (p. 105; see also p. 226). Serves 6.

For the best cumin flavor, lightly toast whole cumin in a dry skillet set over medium-low heat until fragrant. Grind in a spice grinder.

This recipe is also good with a salsa. Choose your favorite brand or one of your own making. Or try Gene's Chipotle Salsa (p. 195).

Cheddar-Crusted Walleye with Gold Garlic Mashers

This is solid walleye comfort food. At home I side this with a fresh green vegetable, freshly baked bread, rolls, or popovers, and a Minnesota brewed ale. In the dining room at Gunflint Lodge, I drizzle two distinctive and colorful sauces over this walleye: a tangy Fire-Roasted Red Pepper Remoulade (p. 226) and a mildly spicy Smoked Yellow Pepper Sauce (p. 226). But these are good "as is" served right on top of the Gold Garlic Mashers.

2½ pounds boneless skinless walleye fillets
9 tablespoons melted butter
Ron Berg's Game-Fish Seasoning to taste (p. 211)
About 2 cups shredded sharp cheddar cheese
About 2 cups dry bread crumbs
Paprika, as needed

Gold Garlic Mashers

2½ pounds Yukon Gold or other yellow-fleshed potatoes, peeled and halved
6 to 8 large cloves of garlic, peeled and halved
4 quarts of cold water seasoned with 1 tablespoon salt
2 to 4 tablespoons soft butter or margarine (optional)
Sour cream as needed (use full fat, light, or non-fat as desired)
Salt and freshly ground black pepper to taste

Preheat oven to 450°F. Melt butter in a small saucepan set over low heat. Spray a shallow-sided baking sheet with nonstick cooking spray. Lay the fillets skin side down in a single layer. Brush fillets with some of the butter and season lightly with Ron Berg's Game Fish Seasoning. Sprinkle a liberal layer of cheddar cheese over the tops of the fillets. Cover the cheese with a handful of dry bread crumbs. Drizzle the crumbs with drops of the remaining butter and sprinkle lightly with paprika. *May be prepared several hours ahead and refrigerated until ready to bake.*

To make the Gold Garlic Mashers, place the potatoes and the garlic in the cold salted water. Bring to a boil over high heat and cook until a fork goes through the potatoes easily. Drain and return to saucepan. Shake the pan with the potatoes over medium-high heat to evaporate remaining moisture. Place potatoes into a bowl and mash, either by hand or with a mixer, adding the optional butter and sour cream as needed to mash to desired consistency. Season to taste with salt and pepper. Cover and keep warm until fish are done.

Bake fish in preheated oven for approximately 5 to 7 minutes or until fish just barely tests done. Serve immediately with Gold Garlic Mashers. Serves 6.

To reheat mashed potatoes, place them in a microwave-able dish and pour a little milk over the top. Cover with plastic film and microwave until hot. Stir the milk into the potatoes and serve.

Walleye with Green Chile Stuffing and Desert Paint Sauces

Here is a full-dress, knock-em-dead presentation that looks and tastes so good one of your guests might be moved to spontaneously pen a sonnet in praise of your cooking right there on a napkin at the table. Serve this with a rice pilaf, a green vegetable of your choice, and a chilled bottle of Riesling or sauvignon blanc.

Preheat oven to 425°F. Stuff fish using the Two-Fillet Method on page 200. Top the exposed stuffing with additional Monterey Jack cheese. Bake in preheated oven for 12 to 20 minutes. To serve, use squeeze bottles of Fire-Roasted Red Pepper Remoulade (p. 226) and Smoked Yellow Pepper Remoulade (p. 226) to paint the bottom of a warm plate with a criss-cross pattern. Place fish in center of plate. Sprinkle Tomato Compote and green onion tops around fish. Drizzle the cheese-topped stuffing with decorative squiggles of Green Chile Aioli (p. 227) and Mexican Crema (p. 227). Sprinkle rim of plate with Aromatic Red Chile Rub if desired (recipe below). Serve accompaniments on side dishes.

Aromatic Red Chile Rub

Use as a plate rim garnish for Southwestern dishes or as a seasoning rub for grilled or roasted fish.

    ¼ cup ancho chile powder
    2 tablespoons ground cumin
    ½ teaspoon ground coriander
    1½ teaspoons kosher salt
    Freshly ground black pepper to taste

Combine all ingredients and mix well. Store in an airtight container in a cool dark place.

French-Fried Onion-Crusted Walleye

The crunchy onion crust on this walleye is added near the end of the cooking time and dusted with Parmesan cheese. You'll probably be tempted to reach for the ketchup when you taste this for the first time.

> 1 large yellow onion
> Buttermilk to cover onions
> Northwoods All-Purpose Breading Mix as needed (p. 208)
> 2½ pounds boneless, skinless walleye fillets
> 6 tablespoons butter, melted
> 2 cloves garlic, minced
> Salt and fresh ground black pepper to taste
> Freshly grated Parmesan cheese
> Chopped chives or thinly sliced green onion tops for garnish

Peel and thinly slice onion and separate into rings. Cover with buttermilk and let marinate for 30 minutes to 1 hour. Use a colander to drain onions well, then dredge in breading mix. Shake off excess breading and deep-fry in 360°F oil until crisp and golden. Drain well, cool, and chop the onions, but not too finely. *May be made up to 3 days ahead and refrigerated in an airtight container.*

Preheat oven to 450°F. Combine melted butter and minced garlic. Place walleye fillets skin side down in pans sprayed with nonstick cooking spray. Brush fillets with garlic butter and season lightly with salt and pepper. Bake in preheated oven until fish is a little underdone. Coat top of fillet with the chopped french-fried onions and a light sprinkling of Parmesan cheese. Return to oven for a minute or so to finish cooking and heat up onion topping. Sprinkle with chives or green onion tops and serve with additional grated Parmesan cheese if desired. Serves 6.

Frozen onion rings prepared according to package directions and chopped may be substituted for the homemade ones above. Easier still is to use those crisp fried onions that come in a can.

How Do I Tell When Fish Is Cooked?

Like most chefs, fish is one of my favorite foods to prepare. One reason is that, like chicken, it lends itself to so many variations. It also cooks quickly, which is as much an asset as it is a liability, for it is easily and frequently overcooked.

The all-too-common advice to cook fish until it flakes results in overcooked fish every time. Fish, like all foods, continues to cook after being removed from the heat, a process known as "carryover cooking." A piece of fish that is perfectly cooked in the kitchen will likely be overcooked by the time it reaches the table.

Fish vary greatly in thickness, making any hard and fast rules difficult to formulate. One rule, commonly referred to as the Canadian rule, calls for baking fish for 10 minutes at 450°F for every inch of thickness when measured at the thickest part. This works surprisingly well. A good way to check for doneness with thicker pieces of fish, such as salmon or lake trout, is to gently look between the flakes of the fish. When most of the raw look is gone, the fish is done. Carryover cooking will finish the job by the time the fish is served.

Thinner fillets, such as walleye, bass, northern pike, and the like, cook very quickly. As a general rule, when the outside of the fillet turns opaque, the inside is close to being done.

Another test is to check the thinner part of the fillet. If it flakes, the thicker part should be done. If the thicker part flakes as well, it is overcooked.

When deep-frying fish, use a long skewer or fork to test for doneness. If it goes through the fillet with no resistance, the fish is ready.

Roasted Walleye Fillets with Tomatoes, Quattro Formaggi, and Pesto Sauce

This walleye is topped with ripe red tomatoes and gratinéed with an Italian blend of cheeses before being drizzled with a tangy, bright green, basil pesto sauce.

> 1 cup mayonnaise
> ⅓ cup Basil Pesto (recipe follows)
> ¼ cup cultured buttermilk, more as needed for consistency
> 1 tablespoon fresh lemon juice (or to taste)
> Salt and freshly ground black pepper to taste
> Thinly sliced firm ripe tomatoes (3 to 4)
> 2½ pounds boneless, skinless walleye fillets
> Melted butter, as needed
> Salt and freshly ground black pepper
> 1½ cups (6 ounces) Quattro Formaggi cheese (A blend of four Italian cheeses, usually mozzarella, provolone, Parmesan, and Asiago. Buy a similar blend or substitute a mixture of freshly grated mozzarella and Parmesan and/or Romano.)
> Diagonally cut fresh chives or green onion tops for garnish

Prepare Pesto Sauce by combining the first five ingredients and whisking well. *May be made up to three days ahead and refrigerated.* Bring to room temperature before using. Makes about 1½ cups.

Preheat oven to 450°F. Lay walleye fillets on shallow-sided sheet pan that has been coated with nonstick cooking spray. Brush walleye with the melted butter and season lightly with salt and pepper. *May be prepared ahead and refrigerated for up to an hour.*

Roast walleye in preheated oven for 3 minutes. Remove from oven and lay a slightly overlapping layer of tomato slices over each fillet. Sprinkle a light layer of cheese over tomatoes and return to oven. Continue cooking until cheese is melted and fish are barely cooked through, about 3 to 5 minutes more. Remove from oven and transfer each serving to a heated plate. Drizzle Pesto Sauce over the cheese and sprinkle with diagonally cut fresh chives. Serves 6.

Basil Pesto

    2 cups fresh basil leaves, lightly packed
    2 tablespoons pine nuts or walnuts
    2 cloves garlic, peeled and lightly crushed
    1 teaspoon kosher salt
    ½ cup freshly grated Parmesan cheese
    2 tablespoons freshly grated Romano cheese (optional)
    ¼ to ½ cup extra-virgin olive oil

Combine basil leaves, pine nuts, garlic, salt, and cheeses in blender or food processor with a metal blade. Turn machine on and drizzle in the olive oil. Makes about 1 to 1¼ cups pesto.

Leftover pesto may be refrigerated for 3 to 4 weeks. Pack the pesto into a small container and pour a thin layer of olive oil over the top and cover tightly. The less the pesto is exposed to air, the better the beautiful green color will last and the better it will keep. For long-term storage, freeze the pesto in small containers for up to 6 to 8 months.

Baked Walleye with Tomato-Basil Fondue

Tomatoes, garlic, and basil flavor this concentrated tomato essence, which complements the walleye in this easy company dish.

> 2 tablespoons butter or margarine
> 2 tablespoons chopped onions
> 2 medium firm but ripe tomatoes, peeled, seeded, and diced
> 1 clove garlic, minced (more to taste)
> ¼ cup chopped fresh basil
> 2 tablespoons dry white vermouth or dry white wine
> Salt and freshly ground black pepper to taste
> 2½ pounds boneless, skinless walleye fillets
> ½ cup freshly grated Parmesan cheese

Prepare the Tomato-Basil Fondue: Melt the butter in an 8- or 10-inch skillet set over medium-low heat. When sizzling, add the onions and cook until soft. Add the diced tomatoes and garlic. Reduce heat to low and cook until the juices begin to evaporate and concentrate. Stir in the basil and wine. *May be prepared up to 3 days ahead and refrigerated until needed.*

Preheat the oven to 450°F. Place walleye fillets in one layer in a shallow casserole. Spread the Tomato-Basil Fondue over the top of the fillets. *May be assembled up to 2 hours ahead and refrigerated until ready to bake.*

Bake in preheated oven for 5 minutes, then sprinkle with Parmesan cheese. Return to oven and continue baking for 5 to 7 minutes longer, or until fish barely tests done. Serves 6.

A Midsummer's Eve Gratin of Walleye with Ripe Garden Tomatoes and Cheese

Here is a recipe to showcase the superb flavor of tomatoes fresh from the garden and freshly caught walleyes. The fillets are baked with tomatoes in a wine, mustard, and cream sauce covered with a savory crisp cheese and bread-crumb topping. Enjoy this with a chilled bottle of your favorite sauvignon blanc.

Soft butter as needed

2½ pounds boneless, skinless walleye, whitefish, or other game fish fillets

¼ cup dry white vermouth or dry white wine

¼ cup fish stock or clam juice

½ cup heavy cream

1 tablespoon plus 1½ teaspoons Dijon mustard

Salt and freshly ground black pepper, to taste

3 to 4 firm ripe tomatoes, peeled, seeded, and diced, to measure about
   2 cups

3 tablespoons finely minced onions

6 tablespoons chopped parsley

2 small cloves garlic, finely minced

2¼ cups fresh white bread crumbs

¾ cup freshly grated Parmesan cheese

6 tablespoons melted butter

Preheat oven to 375°F. Butter a shallow baking dish or large oval gratin dish that will just hold the fillets in a slightly overlapping layer. In a medium bowl, whisk together the dry white vermouth or wine, the cream, and the mustard and pour over and around the fillets.

Season fish lightly with salt and pepper and strew the diced tomatoes over the fillets in an even layer. In a medium bowl, combine the onions, parsley, garlic, bread crumbs, Parmesan cheese, and melted butter and mix well. Sprinkle the bread-crumb mixture evenly over the fish and tomatoes. *May be made up to 2 hours ahead. Cover and refrigerate until ready to bake.* Bake for 15 to 30 minutes or so, depending on the thickness of the fillets, or until fish is barely done. Serves 6.

A whole-grain mustard is a nice substitute for the smooth Dijon. If you don't have fish stock or clam juice, you can substitute a light chicken stock (or low-sodium canned) or omit completely and simply increase the cream to ¾ cup. Use a food-processor with a metal blade to prepare the fresh bread crumbs. You may also prepare this in individual gratin dishes if desired.

Walleye Stack with Julienne Vegetables and Dill Sauce

This wine-broiled walleye, layered with butter-braised matchstick-cut (julienne) vegetables and topped with a creamy dill sauce, is colorful ambrosial fare. Side this with wild rice pilaf and a chilled bottle of chardonnay or sauvignon blanc.

3 tablespoons butter
3 tablespoons flour
1 cup white wine fish stock or bottled clam juice
½ cup heavy cream
½ teaspoon Dijon mustard (more to taste)
2 tablespoons chopped fresh dill or 2 teaspoons dried dill weed
Salt and white pepper, to taste
Drops of fresh lemon juice
4 tablespoons butter
1 cup julienned carrots
1 cup julienned celery
1 cup julienned onions
Salt and freshly ground black pepper, to taste
2½ pounds walleye fillets cut into 12 similar-sized pieces
Melted butter as needed
Salt and freshly ground black pepper, to taste
Paprika
Dry white vermouth or white wine, or a mixture of wine and water

To make the sauce, melt the butter in a saucepan set over medium-low heat. Make a roux by whisking in the flour and cooking for 2 minutes without browning, stirring occasionally. Remove from heat and let cool for a minute or so. In a bowl, combine the fish stock or clam juice and cream. Add all at once to the roux and whisk to incorporate. Return pan to medium heat and cook, stirring constantly until the mixture comes to a boil and is thickened and smooth. If too thick, thin with additional fish stock or clam juice. Stir in the Dijon mustard and dill. Season to taste with salt, white pepper, and drops of lemon juice to taste. *May be made up to 2 days ahead and refrigerated covered. Reheat over low heat to serve.*

For the vegetables, melt 4 tablespoons of butter in a 10-inch skillet set over medium heat. When the foaming subsides, add the julienned carrots, celery, and onions and cook, tossing and turning for a minute or two. Reduce heat to low and season lightly with salt and pepper. Cover and sweat the vegetables for about 5 minutes or until they are tender-crisp. Keep warm.

For the walleye, preheat oven to 450°F. Lay walleye pieces skin side down in a shallow-sided pan just large enough to hold the fillets in a single layer. Brush the tops of the fillets with butter. Season lightly with salt and pepper and sprinkle with paprika. Pour vermouth or white wine *around* the fillets to avoid washing off seasonings. Bake in oven for 5 to 8 minutes or until fish just barely tests done.

To assemble, place one piece of walleye in the center of each heated plate. Top the fillet with a portion of the julienned vegetable mixture and place another piece of fish on top of the vegetables. Spoon a ribbon of sauce over the fish. Serves 6.

For this dish it is best to have 6 walleyes of similar size to cut in half. This will make the servings roughly the same. Also, when assembling the plates, try to match up the similar-shaped pieces with each other for best presentation. You can add extra flavor to your sauce by reducing the defatted wine cooking juices in a small skillet set over high heat until syrupy. Strain into sauce.

Wines to Serve with Fish

Serving a good bottle of wine with a meal adds that final touch of elegance to your culinary efforts without adding any work. But choosing a wine to complement a meal can seem daunting, especially when we face row upon row of wines from around the world at the wine shop. Keep in mind that the few suggestions offered below serve only as a very brief introduction to the vast array of wines that are available. My advice is to buy wines you enjoy and can afford, and not to worry about which wine is the "right" wine. It is, after all, a matter of personal taste.

With simple fish dishes, such as those that are broiled, baked, roasted, panfried, or deep-fried, I prefer an inexpensive crisp dry white wine, such as an Italian pinot grigio. The crisp citrus flavors meld well with the fresh clean flavors of the fish. If you have a favorite white wine, it will go well here.

As the flavors of the finished fish dishes get more complex and robust, so should the wine. For everyday drinking I favor a California sauvignon blanc, a dry white wine with herbal overtones, a quality referred to as "grassiness." Sauvignon blanc is a wonderful wine to pair with fish. It goes especially well with fish dishes containing herbs. A more elegant (and expensive) choice would be a French sauvignon blanc, such as Pouilly-Fumé from the Loire region.

Chardonnays are superb with many fish dishes, especially those served with a cream sauce. However, some California chardonnays are a little too oaked for my taste and, in my opinion, are better served as an aperitif than with food. Choose the more lightly oaked California chards (ask your wine merchant for suggestions) or a French chardonnay such as Mâcon-Villages or the more expensive Pouilly-Fuissé.

A common dictum is to serve white wines with fish. While this is generally true, some red wines, the lighter-style reds in particular, go extremely well with some fish dishes. A pinot noir or a slightly chilled Beaujolais wine goes wonderfully well with grilled or smoked salmon or lake trout. These lighter reds are also good to drink with fish dishes that have assertively flavored sauces, such as the Ancho Grilled Lake Trout with Smoked Yellow Pepper Remoulade and Tomato-Basil Salsa (p. 120) or the Bacon-Hazelnut Stuffed Brook Trout with Wild Mushroom Sauce (p. 126).

Because pinot noir complements the earthy flavor of wild mushrooms, I like it with the Opening Day Walleye Fillets with Morel Cream Sauce (p. 118). But I would also enjoy this same dish with a good chardonnay. When it comes to what wine to serve, there are always choices and it is hard to make a wrong one. It bears repeating that the most important rule is to drink the wine you enjoy most.

Champagne traditionally complements spicy and smoked foods. In truth champagne is sort of a universal food wine; if in doubt, you are usually safe serving champagne. I doubt anyone would complain about your choice.

And speaking of spicy fish dishes, a half-dry Riesling wine, such as a German Mosel or Rheingau, can stand up to the heat of chiles and peppers, as well as to fish dishes with sweet-and-sour flavors. California and Oregon produce some fine Riesling wines.

When serving more than one wine at a meal the general rules are to progress from lighter to more full-bodied, cheaper to more expensive, and from whites to reds if serving both. All of these reasons have to do with the interactions of the wines with each other. If, for example, you were to serve a very expensive and very fine wine with the first course, any less expensive wines that followed would taste very cheap indeed by comparison.

Walleye Stuffed with Salmon Mousseline on a Bed of Spinach with Champagne Sauce

The perfect wine to serve with this elegant entrée would be, of course, champagne.

> ½ pound boneless, skinless salmon, cut into 1-inch chunks
> 1 egg white
> ½ teaspoon salt
> ⅛ teaspoon white pepper
> Speck nutmeg
> 1 cup cream
> 6 6- to 8-ounce walleye fillets or 12 3- to 4-ounce walleye fillets
> Melted butter, as needed
> Salt to taste
> 1 10-ounce package fresh spinach
> 1 tablespoon butter
> Salt and freshly ground black pepper
> ½ recipe Champagne Sauce (p. 220)

To make the salmon mousseline, combine the salmon chunks and the egg white in a food processor fitted with a metal blade. Process until pureed to a paste. Add the salt, white pepper, and nutmeg. With the processor running, slowly add the cream and process for an additional 6 to 8 seconds. Cover and refrigerate immediately. *May be made several hours ahead and refrigerated covered.*

Stuff the walleye fillets using the Casserole Method if using 6- to 8-ounce fillets, or the Two-Fillet Method if using the smaller fillets (see "How to Stuff a Fish," p. 200). *May be stuffed up to 2 hours ahead and refrigerated lightly covered with plastic film.*

Sort the spinach, removing any blemished leaves and the coarse stems. Plunge leaves up and down in cold water, shake lightly, and place in a large pot set over medium heat. Cover and steam in just the water clinging to the leaves for 3 to 5 minutes or until wilted. Do not overcook. The leaves should still be bright green. Drain cooked spinach in a colander, pressing with a large spoon to remove excess water. Turn spinach onto a cutting board and chop coarsely. Scrape chopped spinach into a bowl and toss with butter, salt, and pepper to taste. *May be made up to 15 minutes ahead and kept warm. If you keep it warm for too long, you risk losing the bright green color. The cooked seasoned spinach may also refrigerated for up to 2 days and reheated in the microwave in a microwave-safe dish just before serving.*

To serve, preheat oven to 425°F. Brush fish with melted butter and season lightly with salt. Pour about a ¼ inch of white wine or white wine and water around the stuffed fillets. Bake in preheated oven for 15 to 20 minutes or until fish are just done. Place equal portions of the spinach on 6 heated plates. Place a stuffed fish portion on top of each bed of spinach and top with a ribbon of the Champagne Sauce. Serves 6.

In a small skillet set over medium-low heat, fry up a small amount of the salmon mousseline and taste for seasoning. Add additional salt and white pepper to taste.

Use a pastry bag fitted with a number 9 fluted tip to pipe the mousseline onto the fillets for a nice presentation.

Opening Day Walleye Fillets with Morel Cream Sauce

On opening day some years ago, I happened upon a patch of morel mushrooms on the shore of the central Minnesota lake I was fishing. The following recipe resulted from that fortunate find. Now that fresh farm-raised morels are now commercially available, you can enjoy this dish all year around.

> 3 tablespoons butter, melted
> 2 teaspoons freshly squeezed lemon juice
> 4 6- to 8-ounce boneless, skinless walleye fillets
> Salt and pepper to taste
> Paprika
> ½ cup dry white wine
> 12 fresh morel mushrooms (substitute 1 ounce dried morels—directions below)
> 1¼ cups heavy cream
> Freshly chopped chives or parsley

Preheat oven to 450°F. Combine butter and lemon juice. Place walleye fillets skin side down on a baking sheet. Brush with lemon butter. Season lightly with salt, pepper, and paprika. Pour wine around the fillets. Bake on top rack of oven for 4 to 6 minutes or until fish is just barely done. Remove fillets with a long spatula to a heated serving platter. Cover with foil to keep warm while making the sauce.

Pour remaining juices and butter into a medium skillet. Bring to a simmer over medium heat. Add morels (halved if large). Cook, tossing and turning until they soften and give up their juices. Increase heat to high. Cook until wine and mushroom juices are reduced to a couple of tablespoons. Add cream. Boil rapidly until reduced to a saucelike consistency, about 4 to 5 minutes. Add any juices that have accumulated around fillets to sauce. Continue cooking for 30 seconds. Remove from heat. Season to taste with salt, pepper, and drops of lemon juice. Spoon sauce over fillets. Sprinkle with chives or parsley. Serves 4.

To use dried morel mushrooms, soak 1 ounce dried morels in ¾ cup boiling water for 30 minutes. Remove mushrooms and strain the soaking liquid. In a small saucepan reduce the soaking liquid to 2 tablespoons and add to sauce along with the wine. Add the reserved morels when adding the cream.

Ancho Grilled Lake Trout with Smoked Yellow Pepper Remoulade and Tomato-Basil Salsa

Lake trout is best enjoyed fresh or shortly after freezing. Salmon is an easily purchased and excellent substitute for the trout. The Ancho Grill Rub and the Smoked Yellow Pepper Remoulade are versatile and as delicious on grilled pork and chicken as they are on fish. The rub is mildly spicy and the remoulade is as spicy or as mild as you want, depending on the amount of chipotles you add. Leftover chipotles *en adobo* may be frozen in small batches for future use.

Smoked Yellow Pepper Remoulade

2 smoked yellow peppers, peeled and seeded (smoking directions on p. 175)
1⅓ cups mayonnaise
Juice of ½ lime (or to taste)
½ chipotle *en adobo*, minced plus ½ teaspoon *adobo* sauce (or to taste)
Salt and freshly ground black pepper to taste

Tomato-Basil Salsa

2 ripe but firm tomatoes, diced
2 tablespoons red onion, finely diced
1 tablespoon jalapeño pepper, seeded and minced
3 to 4 tablespoons balsamic vinegar (or to taste)
½ cup fresh basil chiffonnade
1 tablespoon olive oil
Salt and freshly ground black pepper to taste

2½ pounds lake trout or salmon fillets, cut into 6 pieces
Ancho Grill Rub, as needed (recipe below)
Diagonally sliced green onion tops

For the Smoked Yellow Pepper Remoulade, combine all ingredients in a food processor with a metal blade and puree. Taste for seasoning. Put through a fine strainer. *May be made up to 2 weeks ahead and stored in the refrigerator.* Put in plastic squeeze bottle to use.

Make the Tomato-Basil Salsa shortly before grilling fish by combining all ingredients and tossing together.

Build a charcoal fire on both sides of a covered kettle grill according to the manufacturer's instructions for an indirect fire. Sprinkle both sides of the salmon fillets with Ancho Grill Rub. Working in batches, grill the fillets, flesh side down, over the hot coals on the sides of the grill until marked and lightly browned, then turn over so the skin side is down and in the middle of the grill. When all the fillets are marked and lined up in the middle, cover grill and cook until fish test barely done.

Remove to individual warm serving plates and drizzle the top of each serving with a decorative squiggle of the Smoked Yellow Pepper Remoulade and some of the sliced green onion tops. Spoon some of the salsa around each serving and serve the rest on the side. Serves 6.

Ancho Grill Rub

½ cup ancho chile powder
2 tablespoons ground cumin
1½ teaspoons granulated garlic
1 teaspooon ground coriander
2 tablespoons Gunflint Steak and Chop Seasoning (p. 39)
Several grinds black pepper
1 teaspoon sugar

Combine all ingredients and mix well. Store in shaker in a cool dry place.

Roasted yellow peppers may be substituted for the smoked yellow peppers. If a smoky taste is desired, a drop or two of liquid smoke may be added to the sauce.

To make a basil chiffonade, stack 2 or 3 basil leaves, one on top of another, and roll them up lengthwise. Use a sharp knife to slice off thin "ribbons" of the basil. Repeat as necessary.

Roast Brook Trout with Chive Hollandaise Sauce

Also referred to as speckled trout or just "brookies," Minnesota's only native trout is wonderful eating, as are all stream trout. This is a favorite trout recipe.

> 6 small whole brook trout or other stream trout
> 2 tablespoons melted butter mixed with 2 teaspoons fresh lemon juice
> 1 lemon, thinly sliced
> 1 small onion, thinly sliced
> Salt and freshly ground black pepper to taste
> Chive Hollandaise Sauce (p. 233)

Preheat oven to 450°F. Place trout in shallow-sided baking sheet. Brush fish inside and out with butter and lemon juice mixture and season to taste with salt and pepper. Place a layer of thinly sliced onions and lemons in the cavity and on top of the trout.

Bake fish for approximately 10 minutes per inch of fish measured at the thickest part. Baste occasionally with any remaining lemon butter. Remove all lemon and onion slices from the trout and discard. Serve with Chive Hollandaise Sauce. Serves 6.

Simple Surgery: Removing Bones from Trout

Small trout are usually gutted, gilled, and cooked whole with the head on. If the head bothers you, it may be removed either before or after cooking. The bones may also be removed either before or after cooking. Many people, myself included, believe that the bones contribute a succulent flavor to the cooked fish and should be left in whenever possible. When stuffing a whole fish, however, I prefer to remove the bones for easier eating. Here in a nutshell is a guide to removing the bones from both cooked and uncooked trout or any whole fish.

To remove the bones from a whole cooked trout, use two forks or a knife and a fork to separate the top fillet from the backbone and ribs. Use your utensils to flip the top fillet over onto its skin side. Now use a napkin or two forks to grab the head (or the backbone if the head has been removed) of the trout and lift. All the bones will lift away from the bottom fillet and you will have two boneless fillets remaining.

Boning an uncooked trout is a little more involved, but the effort is worth it. You will need a thin, bladed, sharp knife, such as a paring or fillet knife. Begin by placing the gutted and gilled trout with the body cavity up. Beginning by the head, slide the blade of the knife behind the ribcage with the cutting edge facing up. Hold the knife blade close to the ribs and slice upward from the backbone to free the ribs from the flesh. Continue cutting down toward the tail until all the ribs are free. Continue cutting down along the backbone to the tail, freeing it without cutting through the skin of the back. Next cut through the backbone at the tail end. A kitchen shears works well for this. Then lift the back bone to free it from the fish until you reach the head. You may need to do some cutting with the knife to do this, especially by the dorsal fin area. Then use a kitchen shears or your knife to sever the backbone where it connects to the head. *Voilà!* Boneless trout! This method can be used with any fish of any size that is to be baked and stuffed. Use the bones to make a fine fish fumet or stock (p. 216), which, in turn, can be turned into a sumptuous sauce to serve with the fish.

Lake Trout with Ham, Leeks, and Orange-Butter Sauce

This combination of flavors has to be tasted to be believed: first slivers of leeks are braised with julienned sticks of smoky ham in orange juice and chicken stock, then the liquid is reduced to concentrate flavors and butter is whisked in to make a richly flavored sauce. The trout is braised in white wine and orange juice, then topped with the braised leeks and ham, which have been moistened with the sauce.

½ cup julienned leeks, white part only
½ cup julienned smoked ham
½ cup orange juice, fresh or from concentrate
⅓ cup light chicken stock, homemade or low-sodium canned
1½ teaspoons white wine vinegar
5 ounces unsalted butter (1 stick plus 2 tablespoons) cut into 10 pieces
Salt and white pepper to taste
2½ pounds lake trout fillets
Melted butter, as needed
Salt and freshly ground black pepper
White wine and orange juice (or white wine only, if preferred)
Chopped fresh chives
6 orange slices

In a nonreactive skillet set over high heat, combine leeks, ham, orange juice, chicken broth, and white wine vinegar. Bring to a boil and reduce by half. Remove leeks and ham with a slotted spoon and reserve. Continue reducing liquid until syrupy. Whisk in butter all at once. Whisk continuously until just a few pieces of butter remain unmelted. Remove from heat and whisk until remaining butter melts and sauce is smooth and creamy. Season to taste with salt and white pepper. Strain into a 1-pint thermos that has been preheated with hot water. *Sauce may be made up to 2 hours ahead.*

Preheat oven to 450°F. Lay trout skin side down in a shallow-sided sheet pan. Brush the tops of the fillets with melted butter and season lightly with salt and pepper. Pour equal parts white wine and orange juice or just white wine around the fillets to a depth of about ¼ inch. Bake for 10 to 15 minutes or until trout is just done.

To serve, place a portion of trout on each heated plate. Top each portion with some of the reserved leeks and ham. Drizzle with the orange sauce and garnish with chopped chives and an orange twist. Serves 6.

Gunflint Croutons

These are the homemade croutons we serve on our Caesar salads in the dining room at the Gunflint Lodge. I use the leftover crumbs as a primary ingredient in several stuffing recipes. Lacking enough leftover crumbs, the finished croutons may be reduced to coarse crumbs by pulsing them in a food processor with a metal blade. Seasoned bread crumbs or crushed croutons from the store may be substituted for the homemade.

> ¼ pound (1 stick) butter, melted
> ¾ teaspoon onion powder
> ¾ teaspoon granulated garlic
> ¾ teaspoon Italian herb seasoning
> ½ teaspoon celery salt
> 2 quarts French or Italian bread (crusts included) cut into ¾-inch
>   cubes (about half of a 1-pound loaf)

Preheat oven to 300°F. Add seasonings and herbs to melted butter and whisk well to combine. Place cubed bread in a large bowl and drizzle melted butter and seasoning mixture over bread, tossing to mix well. Spread bread out on a large sheet pan in a single layer and bake in preheated oven for 1 to 1½ hours, stirring once or twice, until bread cubes are crunchy throughout, with no soft spots in the middle. *May be made several weeks ahead and stored in an airtight container in a cool area.* Makes about 6 cups croutons.

Bacon-Hazelnut Stuffed Brook Trout with Wild Mushroom Sauce

This dish brings to mind a Minnesota trout stream meandering through cool woods in late summer. If luck were with us, we might find there the simple ingredients to make this dish: a freshly caught stream trout laid to rest on a bed of moss in the creel, a pocketful of wild hazelnuts, and a few precious handfuls of chanterelle or other wild edible mushrooms.

Wild Mushroom Sauce

3 tablespoons butter
2 cups fresh shiitake, oyster, chanterelle, or morel mushrooms, or a mixture of wild mushrooms, sliced
1 cups white mushrooms, sliced
¼ cup chardonnay (or other dry white wine or dry white vermouth)
1½ cups light chicken stock, homemade or low-sodium canned
1 small onion, diced
2½ tablespoons flour
2½ tablespoons butter
¼ cup heavy cream
Salt or a good quality chicken base to taste
Freshly ground black pepper to taste

Bacon-Hazelnut Stuffing

¼ cup chopped crisp bacon
4 to 6 tablespoons chopped, toasted, skinned hazelnuts
1 cup crushed Gunflint Crouton crumbs (p. 125) or your favorite brand of seasoned bread crumbs or croutons

6 whole brook trout or other small whole trout with ribs and backbone removed (p. 4)
6 tablespoons melted butter
Salt and freshly ground black pepper to taste

For the mushroom sauce: In a large skillet set over medium-low heat, melt the butter and add the mushrooms. Toss to coat with butter, then cover the pan and allow the mushrooms to sweat, giving up their juices. Then remove cover and continue cooking until almost dry. Set aside while making the rest of the sauce.

Meanwhile in a saucepan set over high heat, reduce the chardonnay wine by half. Add the chicken stock and onions, reduce heat to medium-low, and simmer for 30 minutes.

Make a roux by melting the 2½ tablespoons of butter in a small pan set over low heat and whisking in the 2½ tablespoons of flour. Cook without browning for a minute or two, then cool completely. Scrape the cooled roux into the simmering chicken stock and whisk vigorously to incorporate. Increase heat to medium-high and whisk constantly until mixture thickens and comes to a boil. Reduce heat to medium and whisk in the cream. If the sauce is too thick at this point, it may be thinned with additional chicken stock. If it is too thin, simmer over medium heat until reduced to a saucelike consistency. Season to taste with chicken base or salt and black pepper. Strain sauce into mushrooms and simmer over low heat for 15 minutes to blend flavors. *May be made up to 3 days ahead and refrigerated or frozen for longer storage. Reheat slowly to use.* Keep warm while roasting trout.

For the stuffing: Combine the bacon, hazelnuts, and crouton crumbs and mix well. *May be made several days ahead and refrigerated until needed.*

Preheat oven to 450°F. Open up trout and brush the cavity with the melted butter. Season lightly with salt and pepper. Sprinkle about ¼ cup of the stuffing mixture into the cavity of each fish and close fish.

Place trout in a shallow pan and brush top of fish with additional butter. Season lightly with salt and pepper. Roast for about 10 to 20 minutes or until the back fin pulls out easily with some meat attached to the bones. Remove top skin if desired, and serve with the Wild Mushroom Sauce spooned over. Serves 6.

To toast and skin hazelnuts (filberts), preheat oven to 350°F. Place 1 cup of hazelnuts in a pie tin and roast in preheated oven for 15 to 20 minutes or until the flesh of the nuts is lightly browned. While still hot, place nuts on the lower half of a large kitchen towel. Fold top half of towel over the nuts. Use the palms of your hands to roll the nuts back and forth between the towel to remove the skins. Don't worry if the skins aren't completely removed. Cool before chopping. Store in an airtight container in a cool, dry place.

Roast Trout Stuffed with Lobster and White Wine Sauce

This is an elegant roast trout dressed with lobster meat and a fine rich sauce. Serve this with mashed potatoes and fresh asparagus, if available. Now is the time to open that expensive bottle of champagne or chardonnay you have been saving for the right occasion. This is that occasion.

9 to 12 ounces cooked lobster meat, fresh, thawed from frozen, or canned
3 cups soft fresh bread crumbs
1½ ribs celery, finely chopped
⅓ cup finely chopped onions
3 tablespoons butter or margarine
6 tablespoons water
3 tablespoons parsley, minced
About 3 to 6 tablespoons heavy cream
Salt and white pepper to taste
2 to 3 dashes hot pepper sauce (or to taste)
1 to 2 dashes Worcestershire sauce (or to taste)
Drops of fresh lemon juice to taste (optional)
1 recipe (about 2¼ cups) White Wine Sauce (p. 218)
Chopped parsley or chives for garnish
6 8-ounce whole boneless trout
Melted butter, as needed
Salt and freshly ground black pepper to taste

Bone out the trout (p. 123), reserving the bones if desired for use in stock (see note at end of recipe). Refrigerate until needed.

To make the lobster stuffing, coarsely chop the lobster meat in a food processor with a metal blade. Mix the chopped lobster and bread crumbs with a fork and refrigerate. Combine the celery, onions, butter, and water in a skillet over moderate heat and simmer until celery is soft and all the water is boiled away. Add to the lobster–bread crumb mixture along with the parsley. Toss to mix. Stir in just enough cream to bind the mixture together. It should still appear crumbly, but will hold together if molded in the hand. Season to taste with salt, pepper, hot pepper sauce, Worcestershire sauce, and the optional lemon juice. Refrigerate 1 to 2 hours until cold. *Stuffing may be made up to 2 days ahead and refrigerated or frozen for up to 3 months.*

Dividing the stuffing evenly, stuff the cavities of each trout. Place on greased baking sheet. Brush the tops of each stuffed trout with melted butter. Season with salt and pepper to taste. Follow the 10-minute rule, baking the trout in a 450°F degree oven for 10 minutes per each inch of thickness measured at the thickest part. Carefully remove the dorsal fin and the top layer of skin. Top the trout with some of the white wine sauce and serve the remainder on the side. Sprinkle the trout with chopped parsley or chives. Serves 4.

The trout bones and trim may be used to make the following enhanced quick fish stock, which can be substituted for the fish stock called for in the Fish Velouté recipe on p. 218.

In a saucepan set over high heat, combine the trout bones and trim with ½ cup dry white vermouth or dry white wine and reduce by half. Add 3 7-ounce bottles clam juice. Bring to a simmer, then reduce heat to low and simmer slowly for 20 to 30 minutes. Strain through a fine sieve and measure out 2 cups of liquid.

Asian Roasted Salmon with Sesame Crust, Ginger Beurre Blanc, and Tomato Concassé

One summer I had the pleasure of working with a talented young chef named Jerry Swanson. We developed the following recipe for salmon, but walleye or lake trout would be equally as delicious.

Ginger Beurre Blanc

½ cup dry white wine
2 tablespoons white wine vinegar
1 tablespoon minced fresh ginger, peeled or not
1 tablespoon minced garlic
1 tablespoon minced shallots
¼ cup heavy cream
12 tablespoons (1½ sticks) unsalted butter, cut into 12 pieces
Salt and cayenne pepper to taste

Asian Marinade and Baste

¼ cup vegetable oil
¼ cup Asian fish sauce
2 tablespoons soy sauce
About 1½ teaspoons fresh lime juice (or to taste)
¾ teaspoon sesame oil (or to taste)
¾ teaspoon oyster sauce or hoisin sauce

Warm Tomato Concassé (chopped tomatoes)

2 Roma tomatoes, peeled, seeded, and cut into ¼-inch dice
1 tablespoon butter
Salt and freshly ground black pepper to taste

½ cup sesame seeds
2½ pounds boneless salmon or other fish fillets
Thinly sliced green onion tops for garnish

Prepare Ginger Beurre Blanc by combining the white wine, vinegar, ginger, garlic, and shallots in a 10-inch skillet set over high heat. Reduce by half, then add cream and again reduce by half. Whisk in butter and when only a few small pieces of butter remain, strain into a bowl. Season to taste with salt and cayenne and blend in a blender or with a hand blender until slightly thickened and fluffy. Pour into warmed thermos. *Sauce will hold in thermos for several hours.*

Make marinade by whisking together the fish sauce, soy sauce, fresh lime juice, sesame oil, and oyster or hoisin sauce. Place fish in a glass, stainless steel, or plastic container (or a plastic bag). Whisk marinade to combine well and spoon about ¼ cup, or more as needed, over the fish to coat. Marinate fish for 45 minutes to 1 hour in the refrigerator. *Any unused marinade can be stored covered in the refrigerator for several weeks.*

Sauté diced Roma tomatoes in a little butter until just warm. Season to taste with salt and pepper. Keep warm.

Toast sesame seeds in a skillet set over medium-low heat, stirring frequently, until lightly browned. Cool and store in an airtight container in a cool place.

To cook fish, preheat oven to 450°F. Calculate approximate cooking time by measuring fish at the thickest part. It takes about 10 minutes to cook a 1-inch thick piece of fish. A ¾-inch thick piece of salmon would take approximately 6 to 8 minutes to cook, depending on how well you want it cooked.

Remove fish from the marinade and place in a single layer in a shallow-sided sheet pan. Pour dry white wine around fish to a depth of ¼ inch. Bake in preheated oven for about half of estimated cooking time. Remove fish from oven and sprinkle toasted sesame seeds liberally over the top of the fish. Return to oven until fish just barely tests done. (Remember the fish will continue cooking for a minute or two after being removed from the oven.) Serve on a pool of the beurre blanc. Top fish with a dollop of warm tomato concassé and thinly sliced green onion tops. Serves 6.

The marinated fish can also be grilled. Start grilling with the skin side up. Sprinkle with the toasted sesame seeds after turning.

Sesame seeds may also be toasted in a 350°F oven for 10 to 15 minutes or until lightly browned.

Roast Rainbow Trout Stuffed with Fresh Garden Herbs and Chive Beurre Blanc

This ambrosial roast whole rainbow trout is stuffed with fresh herbs from the garden and served with a fresh chive beurre blanc.

> 6 tablespoons butter, melted
> 2 cloves garlic, minced
> ½ cup fresh basil, coarsely chopped
> ¼ cup chopped chives or green onion tops
> ¼ cup coarsely chopped flat leaf parsley
> 1½ cups crushed Gunflint Crouton crumbs (p. 125) or your favorite brand
>   of seasoned bread crumbs or croutons
> 6 10-ounce whole boneless trout
> Salt and freshly ground black pepper to taste
> 1 recipe Ron's Beurre Blanc (p. 234)
> 2 to 3 tablespoons chopped chives

Preheat oven to 450°F. Combine garlic and butter. To make the Fresh Garden Herb stuffing, toss together the basil, chives or green onion tops, and the parsley. Open trout and brush with garlic butter. Season lightly with salt and freshly ground pepper. Sprinkle one side of the cavity with about two tablespoons of the herb mixture, then with 3 tablespoons of the crouton crumbs. Close fish and brush with remaining garlic butter. Bake trout in a 450°F oven for about 10 minutes per each inch of thickness measured at the thickest part. Carefully remove the dorsal fin and the top layer of skin. Just before serving, combine the chives and beurre blanc in a warm bowl and spoon a ribbon of the sauce over the trout. Serve remaining sauce on the side. Serves 6.

If you like, the crouton crumbs can be omitted and the trout stuffed with the herb mixture alone. Fresh white bread crumbs may also be substituted for the crouton crumbs.

Salmon with Champagne-Basil Cream

This makes a beautiful presentation with the pinkness of the salmon contrasting with the lovely green basil cream.

2½ pounds salmon fillets, cut into 6 portions
About 5 to 6 tablespoons melted butter
Salt and freshly ground black pepper to taste
2 tablespoons butter
2 small cloves garlic, finely chopped
2½ tablespoons finely chopped shallots
1 cup champagne (substitute dry white wine)
1¼ cups heavy cream
½ to ¾ cup loosely packed fresh basil leaves
3 tablespoons freshly grated Parmesan cheese
Salt and white pepper to taste
Fresh basil leaves for garnish (optional)

Make the sauce by sautéing the garlic and shallots in the butter in a skillet set over low heat until the shallots are soft and translucent. Add the champagne and increase the heat to high. Reduce until syrupy. Add the cream and continue reducing by one fourth, or until saucelike. Place the basil and Parmesan in a blender container and pour the hot cream mixture over the top. Let sit for 5 minutes, then puree for two minutes on high, adding salt and white pepper to taste. *If not using immediately, store in a small preheated thermos.*

Preheat oven to 450°F. Lay salmon fillet portions in a shallow-sided sheet pan sprayed with nonstick cooking spray. Brush tops of fillets with butter and season lightly with salt and pepper. Bake in preheated oven until done as desired, approximately 5 to 10 minutes.

Serve the salmon fillets on heated plates on top of a pool of the sauce or with a ribbon of sauce poured over the fish. Garnish with fresh basil leaves if desired. Serves 6.

If you attempt to heat the sauce for any length of time, you risk losing the bright green color.

Garlic-Butter Roasted Bass with Romano Crust

To make this even more elegant with a touch of delicious decadence, drizzle each serving with white truffle oil just before serving. Pair this with a fresh fennel or wild mushroom risotto (p. 180), fresh buttered asparagus, and a bottle of lightly oaked chardonnay for an extraordinary feast.

4 tablespoons butter
2 to 3 large cloves of garlic, finely chopped
1 to 2 teaspoons fresh lemon juice (or to taste)
2 ½ pounds smallmouth or largemouth bass fillets (substitute boneless walleye or northern pike fillets)
Salt and freshly ground black pepper
1 ½ cups fine dry white bread crumbs
1 cup grated Romano cheese
White truffle oil or Fire-Roasted Red Pepper Remoulade (p. 226)
Diagonally cut fresh chives or green onion tops

Preheat oven to 450°F. In a small saucepan, melt butter and stir in garlic and lemon juice. Spray a shallow-sided baking sheet with nonstick cooking spray. Lay the fillets skin side down in a single layer. Brush fillets liberally with the garlic-lemon butter and season lightly with salt and pepper. Sprinkle Romano cheese liberally and evenly over the buttered fish fillets. Top with dry bread crumbs and drizzle lightly with drops of some of the remaining garlic-lemon butter. *May be prepared several hours ahead and kept covered in the refrigerator until ready to bake.*

Bake in preheated oven for approximately 5 to 6 minutes or until fish just barely tests done. Serve on warm plates with white truffle oil or the Red Pepper Remoulade drizzled over the fish. Sprinkle each serving with fresh chives or scallions. Serves 6.

On larger fish (2 pounds and up) the pin-bones, which run down the center of the fillet, should be removed. Feel the bones by running a finger down the center of the fillet and remove with a knife by cutting along each side. The bones extend from the head end of the fillet to a point just past where the rib bones end.

Baked Bass Fillets with Shrimp Provençal

The area of Provence lies in the south of France where the waters of the Mediterranean lap its shores. Provençal cuisine relies heavily on tomatoes, garlic, basil, and other ingredients associated with the southern climes of Europe. This recipe works equally well with small-mouth or largemouth bass or lake trout.

> 4 tablespoons butter
> 8 ounces fresh white or crimini mushrooms, sliced
> 6 tablespoons dry white vermouth or dry white wine
> 3 firm ripe tomatoes peeled, seeded, and diced
> 3 cloves garlic, minced
> Pinch of sugar (or to taste)
> Salt and freshly ground black pepper to taste
> 2½ pounds boneless, skinless bass or other game fish fillets
> Salt and freshly ground black pepper to taste
> 6 ounces small, whole, cooked shrimp or larger cooked shrimp cut into
> ½-inch pieces
> Parsley sprigs for garnish

Preheat oven to 400°F. In a 10-inch skillet set over medium heat, melt the butter and add the mushroom slices. Cook the mushrooms, tossing and turning until they soften and give up their juices. Increase heat to high and add the dry white vermouth. Reduce to 1 tablespoon. Add the tomatoes, garlic, and the pinch of sugar and cook for 1 minute. Season to taste with salt and pepper and additional sugar if desired. *May be made up to 3 days ahead and stored in a covered container in the refrigerator.*

Arrange the fish fillets in a shallow buttered baking dish large enough to hold the fish in a single, slightly overlapping layer. Season the fish lightly with salt and pepper. Sprinkle the shrimp over the fillets and spoon the tomato mixture over the shrimp.

Bake uncovered in preheated oven for 15 to 25 minutes or until fish barely tests done. Serve from the baking dish or transfer to a heated serving platter and pour the sauce over the fish. Garnish with parsley sprigs. Serves 6.

Seared Bass Fillets with Fennel Mashed Potatoes, Fennel Jus, and Roasted Tomato Confit

This is an elegant dish. Any game fish fillets may be substituted for the bass. Although at first glance this recipe may appear daunting, much of the preparation may be done ahead of time.

Roasted Tomato Confit

> 1 tablespoon olive oil
> 1 clove garlic, minced
> 1 bay leaf
> 1 fresh sprig thyme, leaves only
> 1 teaspoon sugar (or to taste)
> 8 roasted tomato halves, skins removed, and coarsely chopped (p. 206)
> Salt and freshly ground black pepper to taste

Braised Fennel

> 2 fennel bulbs
> 1½ tablespoons olive oil
> Salt and freshly ground black pepper
> ¼ cup dry white vermouth or dry white wine
> 2 cups chicken stock, homemade or low-sodium canned

Fennel Mashed Potatoes

> 2½ pounds Yukon Gold or red potatoes, cooked in boiling salted water and drained
> 4 tablespoons butter
> Reserved braised fennel
> Heavy cream, as needed
> Salt and freshly ground black pepper to taste

> 2½ pounds boneless smallmouth or largemouth bass fillets
> Salt and freshly ground black pepper
> Vegetable oil, as needed

To make the Roasted Tomato Confit: In a small skillet, heat the olive oil over low heat and stir in the garlic, bay leaf, and thyme.

Sauté slowly until garlic is very soft. Stir in the chopped roasted tomatoes and the sugar and cook over low heat for 10 to 15 minutes, stirring frequently. Remove the bay leaf and season to taste with salt and pepper. Keep warm. *Confit may be made 1 day ahead and chilled, covered. Reheat confit in a 150°F oven before serving.*

To braise the fennel: Trim stalks flush with fennel bulbs and cut a thin slice off the base. Cut the bulb lengthwise into quarters. Toss the fennel with olive oil to coat. Place in a shallow roasting pan and season lightly with salt and pepper. Roast at 325°F until lightly browned, about 20 minutes. Add the wine and return to oven. Roast until wine is nearly gone, about 10 minutes. Pour the chicken stock around the fennel and roast until fennel is tender, another 15 to 25 minutes. *Fennel and broth may be made 1 day ahead and refrigerated in a covered container. Reheat fennel in broth before proceeding with recipe.* Drain the fennel, reserving the braising liquid.

To make the potatoes: Return the drained potatoes to the pan and shake over high heat to evaporate any remaining liquid and place in a large warm bowl. In a food processor with a metal blade, puree the reserved fennel. Mash the potatoes with the butter, fennel puree, and enough cream for consistency. Season to taste with salt and black pepper. Cover and keep warm.

Make the fennel jus by boiling the braising liquid until reduced by ½. Season to taste with salt and pepper and keep warm.

Pour an ⅛-inch layer of vegetable oil in a large skillet set over medium-high heat. When the oil is hot but not smoking, season the bass fillets lightly with salt and pepper and lay skin side up in the oil. Fry until nicely browned and turn. Reduce heat to medium-low and continue cooking until just barely done. Remove fish to paper towels to drain.

To serve, divide the potatoes among 6 heated plates and lay a portion of fish over the potatoes. Drizzle the fennel jus over and around the fish and potatoes. Place small spoonfuls of Roasted Tomato Confit around the fish and potatoes. Serves 6.

Northern Pike with Champagne-Tomato-Basil Sauce

A creamy tomato-and-basil-infused champagne sauce complements the rich flavor of northern pike perfectly. Serve this with your favorite sauvignon blanc or champagne.

    2 teaspoons butter
    2 teaspoons minced onions
    1¾ teaspoons minced garlic
    ½ cup champagne or dry white wine
    ½ cup fish stock, clam juice, or light chicken stock
    ¼ teaspoon dill weed
    ¾ cup heavy cream
    Salt and white pepper to taste
    Julienned tomatoes from one ripe tomato (directions below)
    2 tablespoons fresh basil chiffonade (or to taste)
    2½ pounds northern pike or other game fish fillets cut into 6 serving-size
        pieces
    Melted butter as needed
    Salt and freshly ground black pepper to taste
    Dry white wine or vermouth

Sauté onions and garlic in butter for 30 seconds. Add wine and fish stock. Reduce over high heat by one half. Add cream and reduce to saucelike consistency, about 3 to 5 minutes. Strain and season to taste with salt and white pepper. *May be made up to 3 days ahead and refrigerated covered. Reheat gently to serve.* Just before serving, add tomatoes and basil.

Preheat oven to 450°F. Place northern pike fillets in one layer in a shallow casserole. Brush the tops of the fillets with melted butter and season with salt and pepper. Pour dry white wine or vermouth around the fish. Bake in preheated oven for 5 to 10 minutes, depending on thickness of fillets, or until fish barely tests done.

Use a slotted spatula to remove fish to heated serving plates or a large platter. Spoon the Tomato-Basil Sauce over and serve immediately. Serves 6.

To julienne tomatoes, cut slices off the sides of a tomato following the curvature of the tomato. Scrape off any seeds attached to the slices. Lay the slices with the skin side down and slice thinly into long strips.

To make a basil chiffonade, stack 2 or 3 basil leaves, one on top of another, and roll them up lengthwise. Use a sharp knife to slice off thin "ribbons" of the basil. Repeat as necessary.

Catfish Creole

Walleye Creole was a popular restaurant dish in Minnesota during the 1970s when it was far easier to get walleye than catfish. Catfish is now available commercially and is perfect for this Louisiana-style dish. Walleye or any game fish is still an excellent substitution for the catfish. You can make the sauce as spicy as you want by adjusting the amount of hot pepper sauce. Serve with white rice and a green salad.

2 tablespoons vegetable oil
2 small cloves garlic, minced, about ¾ teaspoon
½ cup chopped green pepper
½ cup chopped celery
4 ounces sliced mushrooms
1 cup chopped onions
1 28-ounce can whole tomatoes, undrained and chopped
1 bay leaf
½ teaspoon Ron's Creole seasoning (p. 213)
1 tablespoon chopped parsley (optional)
Large pinch of sugar (more as needed)
Salt to taste
Hot pepper sauce to taste
2½ pounds catfish fillets or other boneless game fish fillets
Nonstick cooking spray, as needed
Chopped parsley for garnish

To make the sauce, sauté garlic in butter. Add peppers, mushrooms, and onions. Cover and sweat until vegetables are tender. Add chopped tomatoes with juice, bay leaf, and Creole seasoning and cook over low heat, stirring occasionally, for about 15 to 20 minutes. Add a pinch or two of sugar if sauce tastes acidic. Season to taste with salt and hot pepper sauce. Remove bay leaf and discard. *May be made 3 days ahead to this point and refrigerated, covered, until needed.*

To prepare, preheat the oven to 400°F. Spray nonstick cooking spray on the bottom of a casserole or cake pan large enough to hold the catfish fillets in a slightly overlapping layer. Lay the fish skin-side down in the pan and spread a generous layer of Creole sauce over the fish. Bake in preheated oven for 10 to 15 minutes or until fish is just barely done. Remove with a long spatula to a heated serving platter or to plates. Sprinkle the top with parsley. Serves 6.

Cajun Catfish and Linguine

This Cajun pasta dish can be made as spicy as you like by varying the amount of Cajun seasoning. If you like it on the mild side, you will probably have to add a little salt to taste. Any boneless game fish (even shrimp or scallops) may be substituted for the catfish.

2 teaspoons butter
¼ cup julienned onions
4 ounces boneless, skinless catfish, cut into 1-inch cubes
1½ teaspoons Cajun seasoning (p. 212), more or less to taste
Water, as needed
⅓ cup diced seeded tomatoes
2 tablespoons diagonally sliced green onion tops
4 ounces dry linguine, cooked al dente (see note below)
Salt to taste
1 tablespoon chopped fresh parsley (optional for garnish)

In a medium skillet set over medium heat, melt butter. Add onions and Cajun seasoning to taste and about 2 to 3 tablespoons of water. Sauté, stirring occasionally, until onions turn transparent. Add catfish cubes and stir constantly until the fish loses its raw look and is almost cooked through. Add tomatoes and green onion tops and sauté for an additional 30 seconds.

Reheat the cooked pasta (see note below) and add to the skillet. Remove skillet from heat and toss pasta with the catfish mixture to combine, seasoning to taste with salt. Turn pasta out onto a heated plate or pasta bowl and sprinkle with the optional parsley. Makes 2 appetizer servings or 1 entrée serving.

Pasta may be cooked several hours or even a day or two ahead of time. Cook pasta according to the package directions, making sure the pasta is cooked al dente (still a little firm in the middle). Drain and return to the pan. Run cold tap water over pasta until perfectly cold. Drain and place in a bowl. Toss pasta with olive or vegetable oil to coat. Store covered in the refrigerator until ready to use.

Pasta can be reheated in several ways. An easy restaurant method is to put the amount of pasta you need into a colander or sieve. Lower into a pan of simmering water for a minute or so until pasta is hot. Remove, drain, and serve.

Pasta may also be reheated in a microwave, but be careful. A few seconds too long will result in rubbery pasta.

Always serve pasta on heated plates.

Seared Whitefish with Tuscan White Beans, Spinach Salad, and Tomato-Chive Vinaigrette

The combination of flavors and textures in this Mediterranean-style dish is superb. Serve with a loaf of crusty bread or focaccia sided with extra-virgin olive oil seasoned with freshly ground black pepper, balsamic vinegar, or freshly grated Parmesan cheese to dip it in.

White Beans

1½ cups navy beans soaked overnight or quick-soaked (Cover with 1½ inches of water and bring to a boil. Boil for 5 minutes, cover, turn off heat, and let sit for 1 hour.)

2 to 3 cloves garlic, coarsely chopped

Chicken stock (homemade or low-sodium canned) to cover beans by 1½ inches

¾ teaspoon salt

2 tablespoons olive oil

1 to 3 cloves garlic, minced, to taste

¾ cup chopped onion

2 to 3 pinches dried sage

¾ cup peeled, seeded, and diced fresh tomatoes, or drained, seeded, canned tomatoes cut in medium dice

Salt and black pepper to taste

Tomato-Chive Vinaigrette

½ cup light chicken stock (homemade or canned low sodium), fish stock, or clam juice

¼ cup champagne or white wine vinegar

2 teaspoons finely minced shallots

½ teaspoon finely minced garlic

1 teaspoon Dijon mustard

¼ cup extra-virgin olive oil

Salt and freshly ground black pepper to taste

1 Roma tomato, seeded and cut into ¼-inch dice

1 to 2 tablespoons chopped chives

3 to 4 cups chiffonade of washed and dried spinach or Swiss chard leaves
2½ pounds skinless, boneless whitefish fillets (substitute walleye or small-
    mouth bass fillets) cut into 6 serving-size portions
Salt and freshly ground black pepper to taste
Olive oil

To prepare beans, cover soaked beans with chicken stock to cover by 1½ inches. Add garlic and salt. Bring to a boil and simmer until tender, about 40 minutes to 1 hour. Meanwhile, in a skillet set over low heat, sauté the garlic, onions, and sage until the onions are soft and translucent. Use a slotted spoon to add the cooked beans to the skillet. Reserve remaining cooking liquid. Stir in diced tomatoes and simmer the beans slowly for 30 minutes, adding water or reserved cooking liquid as needed if too dry. Season to taste with salt and freshly ground black pepper. *May be made up to 3 days ahead and refrigerated.*

Prepare vinaigrette by whisking together the vinaigrette ingredients except for the tomatoes and chives. *May be made up to 3 days ahead and refrigerated. Bring to room temperature before serving.* Just before serving, measure out about ½ cup of the vinaigrette mixture and whisk in the diced tomatoes and chives. Place spinach chiffonade in a bowl and toss with just enough vinaigrette to lightly coat the leaves.

Season whitefish with salt and pepper and in a large heavy-bottomed skillet set over medium-high heat, sear the fillets in olive oil until lightly browned on both sides. To serve, place about ½ cup of the beans in the center of each heated plate. Place the seared whitefish on top of the beans and top each portion of fish with some of the spinach salad. Serves 6.

To make a chiffonade, stack 2 or 3 spinach or Swiss Chard leaves, one on top of another, and roll them up lengthwise. Use a sharp knife to slice off thin "ribbons." Repeat as necessary.

Chapter 6

Favorite Recipes from Minnesota Restaurants and Resorts

As one might expect in a state boasting over 10,000 lakes, game fish is a popular offering on restaurant menus. Walleye, the state fish, is the hands-down favorite. But lake trout, whitefish, and rainbow trout are frequently featured as well. Northern pike also makes an occasional menu appearance. Salmon, which is extensively farmed, is found on menus everywhere.

Many of the restaurants featured lie along Lake Superior's North Shore, where fishing has been an industry since before the turn of the century. Restaurants like the Coho Cafe, the Bluefin Restaurant, and the Angry Trout Cafe take great pride in showcasing the bounty of the big lake on their menus.

Lost Lake Lodge near Brainerd lies in the heart of walleye country and the popular game fish is a prominent feature on their evening menu. In Duluth, Bob Bennett (Bennett's on the Lake) and Patrick Cross (Lake Avenue Cafe) attract discriminating diners with their distinctive and creative fish entrées. And this chapter wouldn't be complete without a recipe from my favorite Twin Cities dining spot, the 510 Restaurant.

Angry Trout Cafe, Grand Marais

Owner George Wilkes

The Angry Trout Cafe, established in 1988, is located on the shore of Lake Superior in the Grand Marais harbor next to a fish market. It is exactly where you would expect to find a restaurant that specializes in fresh Lake Superior fish. A deck allows diners to savor the Angry Trout's excellent fresh organic cuisine outside on the water's edge while watching the gulls wheel over the harbor and listening to the waves roll against the breakwater. The following recipe for grilled fresh fish basted with a lime and tarragon sauce is the Angry Trout's signature entrée.

Grilled Lake Superior Trout

When it is available, the Angry Trout uses fresh, locally netted Lake Superior trout, the leaner ones preferred.

Angry Trout Grilling Sauce

½ cup extra-virgin olive oil
¼ cup freshly squeezed lime juice
¼ cup finely chopped red onion
2 teaspoons dried tarragon
½ to ¾ teaspoon salt
¼ teaspoon white pepper

2½ pounds lake trout fillets, fresh preferred, skinned and deboned

To make the grilling sauce, combine the olive oil, lime juice, red onion, tarragon, salt, and white pepper in a medium bowl and whisk to combine thoroughly. Cut trout into serving-size pieces. For proper grilling, they should be no more than 1 inch thick.

Brush trout fillets with grilling sauce and place skin side up on hot oiled grill. Turn when about half done (5 minutes or so, depending on the heat of your grill and the thickness of the fillets). After turning, brush top of trout with a small amount of additional grilling sauce. Continue cooking until done (approximately 3 to 5 minutes more). Garnish with a sprinkling of fresh chopped tarragon and a slice of lime. Serves 6.

Salmon or other game fish suitable for grilling may be substituted for the lake trout.

Coho Cafe, Tofte

Chef Judi Barsness

Under the talented direction of Chef Judi Barsness, the Coho Cafe has quickly gained a reputation for excellence. Besides their heavenly fish entrées, the Coho is known for its homemade artisan-style breads and award-winning pizzas. These two pasta recipes from the Coho Cafe are variations on a theme.

Coho Salmon with Fresh Basil and Four-Cheese Alfredo Sauce on Spinach Fettuccine

This recipe makes good use of the restaurant's namesake, a Lake Superior coho salmon. Fresh coho salmon fillets are available from a fresh fish market or counter in April, May, and early June. Frozen fillets are available throughout the year, as are fresh, whole, baby coho salmon. Coho salmon may be game fished on the North Shore of Lake Superior throughout the summer and early fall. Other salmon may be substituted for the coho if desired.

3 cups heavy cream
½ cup freshly grated Parmesan cheese
¼ cup freshly grated Romano cheese
¼ cup shredded Asiago cheese
½ cup crumbled goat cheese (chèvre)
1 cup chopped fresh basil
1¼ pounds dry spinach fettuccine (1½ pounds if using fresh pasta)
Salt and freshly ground melange of peppercorns to taste (see note below)
2½ pounds fresh coho or other salmon fillets (6–ounce portions approximately)
Salt to taste
Freshly ground melange of peppercorns to taste (see note below)
2 teaspoons roasted-garlic olive oil
½ cup fresh shiitake mushrooms, stems removes and caps sliced
¼ cup fresh basil chiffonade

To make the sauce, bring cream to a boil in a large heavy saucepan set over high heat. Immediately reduce heat and simmer, uncovered, until thickened to a saucelike consistency, approximately 30 minutes. Whisk in the four cheeses until smooth and let cook an additional 5 minutes. Season to taste with salt and freshly ground peppercorn melange and continue to cook for another 5 minutes. *May be made up to 3 days ahead and refrigerated covered. To serve reheat over very low heat or in the top of a double boiler.*

Just before serving, finish the sauce by stirring in the fresh basil and simmering for a final 3 minutes. Keep sauce warm over very low heat while preparing pasta and fish.

To cook the pasta, bring a large pot of water to a boil. Add salt to taste and fettuccine. Cook until al dente. Drain and set aside.

While pasta is cooking, prepare the salmon. Season the fillets lightly with salt and the freshly ground peppercorn melange. Heat a heavy-bottomed skillet over medium-high heat. Add roasted-garlic olive oil to coat the bottom of the pan. Add fillets quickly and pan sear for 3 to 4 minutes per side or until done as desired. Remove fish from pan and keep warm. Add shiitake mushrooms to pan and quickly sauté until limp.

To serve, make a bed of the spinach pasta on a large pasta plate. Top pasta with a ribbon of the sauce and place salmon fillets on top of pasta and sauce. Drizzle fish with additional sauce, making sure some of the pink-red fillet is visible. Sprinkle with the sautéed shiitakes and garnish with the basil chiffonade. Serves 6.

A melange of 4 peppercorns (black, green, white, and pink) and roasted-garlic olive oil are available at specialty shops and many supermarkets.

To make a basil chiffonade, stack 2 or 3 basil leaves one on top of another, and roll them up lengthwise. Use a sharp knife to slice off thin "ribbons" of the basil. Repeat as necessary.

Walleye Florentine with Confetti Alfredo Sauce

    3 cups heavy cream
    ½ cup freshly grated Parmesan cheese
    ½ cup freshly grated Romano cheese
    ¼ cup shredded Asiago cheese
    ½ cup crumbled goat cheese (chèvre), divided
    1 cup fresh basil chiffonade
    ½ cup diced, seeded Roma tomatoes
    Salt and freshly ground melange of peppercorns to taste (see note below)
    2½ pounds fresh walleye fillets
    Salt to taste
    Freshly ground melange of peppercorns to taste (see note below)
    2 teaspoons roasted-garlic olive oil
    1¼ pounds dry spinach fettuccine
    ¼ cup fresh basil chiffonade, garnish

To make the sauce, bring the cream to a boil in a heavy saucepan set over high heat. Reduce heat to low and simmer, uncovered, until thickened to a saucelike consistency, about 30 minutes. Whisk in the four cheeses and continue whisking until smooth. Simmer for an additional 5 minutes, whisking occasionally. Season to taste with salt and freshly ground peppercorn melange and simmer for 5 minutes more. Keep warm while cooking pasta and fish. *May be made up to 3 days ahead and refrigerated covered. To serve, reheat over very low heat or in the top of a double boiler.*

Just before serving, finish the sauce by stirring in the fresh basil and simmering for a final 3 minutes. Remove from heat and stir in the tomatoes, reserving a small amount for the final garnish.

To cook the pasta, bring a large pot of water to a boil. Add salt to taste and fettuccine. Cook until al dente. Drain and set aside.

While pasta is cooking, prepare the walleye fillets. Heat a heavy-bottomed skillet over medium-high heat. Pour in a thin layer of roasted-garlic olive oil to coat the bottom of the pan. Season the walleye fillets with salt and freshly ground peppercorn melange.

Add fillets skin side down and pan sear for 3 to 4 minutes per side or until nicely browned and just barely done.

To serve, place a portion of the spinach fettuccine on each heated plate and top with a ribbon of the sauce. Place a portion of walleye on top of the pasta and sauce and drizzle with another ribbon of sauce, leaving a border of naked fillet. Sprinkle with reserved Roma tomatoes and garnish with the basil chiffonade. Serves 6.

 A melange of 4 peppercorns (black, green, white, and pink) and roasted-garlic olive oil are available at specialty shops and many supermarkets.

Bluefin Restaurant, Tofte

Chef Tracy Jacobsen

The Bluefin Restaurant, under the capable hands of Chef Jacobsen, has been chosen as Minnesota's favorite resort restaurant by the readers of *Minnesota Monthly* magazine. Here is one of his favorite recipes for preparing the resort's namesake fish. The bluefin herring is greatly prized by North Shore locals and visitors alike.

Panfried Bluefin Herring with Almond-Parmesan Crust

> 6 fresh bluefin herring
> 2 eggs
> 1 cup buttermilk
> 2 cups Japanese bread crumbs (panko flakes)
> 1 cup toasted almonds
> ½ cup freshly grated Parmesan cheese
> 1 teaspoon freshly ground Szechuan peppercorns
> 1 teaspoon ground marjoram
> ½ cup butter

In a food processor with a metal blade, grind the almonds to a fine texture. Add all remaining ingredients except the butter and pulse to combine well. Pour crumb mixture into a pie tin or flat plate and spread out evenly. In a medium bowl, whisk together the eggs and buttermilk and set aside.

Dip herring fillets into egg/buttermilk mixture, then roll in crumb mixture, pressing firmly on both sides to coat well and evenly. Set breaded fillets aside on wax paper.

In a large heavy skillet (such as cast iron), melt butter over medium heat. When butter is melted and begins to brown slightly, add fish to pan. Cook for 3 to 4 minutes per side or until done. Remove to paper towels to drain. Serves 3 to 4.

Bennett's on the Lake, Duluth

Chef and Owner Bob Bennett

Bob Bennett's cooking has been exciting Duluth natives and visitors alike since 1992, when Bob and his wife, Kathy, opened Bennett's Bar and Grill in downtown Duluth. Since then their reputation for fine dining has grown steadily. In 1997 they moved the restaurant to a prime location overlooking Lake Superior in the renovated Fitger's brewery building and changed the name to Bennett's on the Lake. The following recipe is an example of the creative cuisine that makes dining at Bennett's such a pleasurable experience.

Caramelized Salmon

1 teaspoon chopped ginger root
¼ cup balsamic vinegar
¼ cup rice vinegar
¼ cup soy sauce
1 tablespoon Oriental sesame oil
1 tablespoon honey
6 6–ounce salmon fillets
Olive oil, as needed
2 tablespoons brown sugar
1 tablespoon butter

In a large bowl combine ginger root, balsamic and rice vinegars, soy sauce, sesame oil, and honey and mix well. Marinate the salmon fillets in the mixture for 20 minutes in the refrigerator.

Preheat oven to 350°F. Remove salmon fillets from the marinade and sear quickly on both sides in a hot sauté pan filmed with olive oil, in batches if necessary, until nicely browned. Remove fish to a shallow baking dish that has been sprayed with nonstick cooking spray. Top each portion of salmon with about ½ teaspoon of butter cut into bits and sprinkle with about 1 teaspoon of brown sugar. Finish cooking in oven until done as desired and outside is caramelized. Serves 6.

Pancetta-Wrapped Rainbow Trout Stuffed with Caramelized Onions

When I first met Bennett's *sous*-chef, Travis Johnson, I was impressed by the depth of his passion for cooking. I soon discovered that his passion was exceeded only by his considerable talents, which are demonstrated below.

2 tablespoons butter
1 large red onion, julienned
Salt and freshly ground black pepper to taste
6 whole 12– to 14–ounce boneless rainbow trout, heads removed
12 strips pancetta
Olive oil, as needed

In a 10-inch skillet set over medium heat, melt 2 tablespoons of butter. Add the julienned red onions and cook, stirring frequently, until nicely browned. Season to taste with salt and pepper. Remove from heat and cool to room temperature before using.

Spread a layer of caramelized onions along the inside of the cavity of each trout, dividing them evenly. Wrap 2 strips of pancetta around each trout. Don't worry about securing the pancetta with toothpicks; it will shrink and tighten around the fish as you sear it.

Preheat oven to 350°F. In a 10-inch skillet set over medium-high heat, add a drizzle of olive oil to cover the bottom of the pan and sear the pancetta-wrapped trout, in batches, about 3 minutes on each side. As the trout finish searing, remove to a shallow-sided sheet pan. When all the trout have been seared, finish cooking in preheated oven for about 12 minutes, or until the fish are barely done. Serves 6.

Pancetta is an Italian cured bacon that is not smoked. It is available in specialty shops and some supermarkets.

Lost Lake Lodge, Lake Shore

Chef and Owner Kieran Moore

Lost Lake Lodge in the Brainerd Lakes area has been winning praises for its cuisine ever since Kieran Moore, chef and co-owner of the lodge with his brother, Tim, and Tim's wife, Cindy, has been working the range in the lodge kitchen. Here are two of Kieran's favorite ways to prepare Minnesota game fish for the lodge's dining room guests.

Lake Trout Oreganata

> 1 cup white wine
> 1 cup clam juice
> 1 cup water
> 1 cup canned Italian tomatoes, drained and chopped
> 2 tablespoons fresh oregano (or 2 teaspoons dry)
> 4 6- to 8-ounce lake trout fillets
> 2 tablespoons olive oil
> Salt and freshly ground black pepper to taste

Combine wine, clam juice, water, tomatoes, and oregano in a 1½-quart saucepan set over medium-high heat and bring to a boil. Continue boiling for 15 to 20 minutes until sauce thickens, but is still pourable.

Preheat oven to 350°F. Brush a shallow baking pan with 1 tablespoon of the olive oil and place fillets in pan. Brush the fillets with the remainder of the oil and season lightly with salt and pepper. Bake for 12 to 15 minutes or until fish is just barely done. Transfer fish to heated serving plates or a heated serving platter and spoon the sauce over the fish. Serves 4.

Parmesan-Crusted Walleye with Lemon and Capers for Two

½ cup grated fresh Parmesan cheese
½ cup flour
Freshly cracked black pepper to taste (or coarse ground)
2 tablespoons butter
1 tablespoon vegetable oil
2 boneless, skinless walleye fillets, 6 to 8 ounces each
1 lemon, cut into wedges
2 tablespoons capers, drained

In a shallow pan, combine Parmesan and flour. Season flour mixture to taste with cracked pepper. Dredge the flesh side of walleye in the flour mixture, leaving skin side uncoated.

Heat butter and oil in a large sauté pan set over medium heat until the foaming of the butter begins to subside. Sauté the walleye, coated side first, until the crust achieves a golden hue, about 3 minutes. Flip walleye and continue cooking on the uncoated side for another 2 minutes or until just cooked through.

Squeeze drops of fresh lemon juice over the fish and sprinkle with the capers. Serves 2.

Lake Avenue Cafe, Duluth

Chef and Owner Patrick Cross

The Lake Avenue Cafe, located in the Dewitt-Seitz Marketplace in the upscale Canal Park area of Duluth, is one of the city's favorite eating spots. It is owned by Patrick and Mary Ann Cross. Prior to purchasing the restaurant, Patrick had been the executive chef under the previous owners. Today Patrick continues to serve the superb fresh cuisine that has been the hallmark of the Lake Avenue Cafe. This superb recipe for salmon is the restaurant's all-time favorite entrée.

Salmon with Peaches and Berries

> 2 tablespoons butter
> 1 tablespoon vegetable oil
> 1½ teaspoons Dijon mustard
> 1 cup heavy cream
> 2 7- to 8-ounce salmon fillets
> About ½ cup seasoned flour (recipe below)
> 1 cup thickly sliced mushrooms
> 1 ripe peach, sliced into 8 to 10 slices
> 2 tablespoons brandy
> Fresh raspberries (approximately 2 tablespoons)

Preheat oven to 400°F. In a small bowl whisk together the Dijon mustard and heavy cream and set aside while preparing the salmon.

Heat the butter and oil in a sauté pan set over medium-high heat. Dredge salmon fillets in the seasoned flour and sauté 2 to 3 minutes on each side. Remove salmon from pan and place on a sheet pan or pie tin. Finish cooking salmon in preheated oven for 3 to 4 minutes or until done as desired.

As salmon finishes cooking, prepare the sauce. Pour remaining oil from sauté pan and add peaches and mushrooms; sauté for 10 to

15 seconds then add brandy and flambé. Immediately add the mustard cream mixture. Reduce heat to medium and simmer until thickened to a saucelike consistency.

Place salmon on heated serving plates and top with the peach and mushroom sauce. Sprinkle fresh raspberries over the salmon. Serves 2.

Lake Avenue Cafe Seasoned Flour

This makes more than you will need for the recipe above, but the remainder stores well and may be used in any recipe calling for seasoned flour.

2 cups flour
1½ teaspoons paprika
2 tablespoons salt
1½ teaspoons onion powder
¾ teaspoon cayenne pepper
¾ teaspoon white pepper
Pinch of dry mustard
¾ teaspoon chili powder

Combine all ingredients and blend well.

If fresh peaches and raspberries are not in season (which is most of the year in northern Minnesota), Patrick and Mary Ann suggest using individually quick frozen fruit as an excellent substitute for the fresh.

The 510 Restaurant, Minneapolis

Owners Craig and Brad Schutte

The 510 Restaurant, located at 510 Groveland Avenue near downtown Minneapolis, is my personal favorite in the Twin Cities. Not only is the cuisine consistently excellent and reasonably priced (imagine a three-course meal consisting of an appetizer, entrée, and dessert for only $19.95), but the Schuttes are masters of hospitality. The following recipe for this exquisite salmon was one I sampled on a recent visit. It employs a common restaurant technique of using both the grill and the oven.

Citrus-Glazed Salmon with Cilantro-Ginger Beurre Blanc

¼ cup brown sugar
¼ cup honey
½ cup orange juice
¼ cup soy sauce
¼ cup dry white wine
2 tablespoons minced fresh ginger
2 tablespoons minced shallots
¼ pound (1 stick) butter, cut into 8 pieces
1 tablespoon chopped cilantro
Salt and white pepper to taste
4 6- to 8-ounce salmon fillets

Prepare the Citrus Glaze by combining the brown sugar, honey, orange juice, and soy sauce in a medium saucepan. Bring the mixture to a boil and reduce by two-thirds. Set glaze aside to cool and thicken.

Prepare the Cilantro-Ginger Beurre Blanc. In a 10-inch non-reactive skillet combine the white wine, ginger, and shallots. Reduce until pan is almost dry. Reduce heat to medium. Whisk in butter pieces 1 at a time, whisking constantly. When about ½ of the butter has been incorporated, add the remaining pieces 2 at a time. When only a few small pieces of butter remain, remove from heat and whisk until butter pieces melt into the sauce. Season to taste with salt and pepper and whisk in cilantro. Hold the sauce in a bowl set over warm water while preparing the salmon.

To cook, preheat grill and oven broiler. Brush hot grill with a light coating of vegetable oil. Brush some oil on the salmon fillets as well. Grill the salmon to medium-rare (fish will continue to cook under broiler). Remove salmon from grill and place in a shallow-sided pan large enough to hold the salmon fillets without crowding. Brush the salmon fillets with the glaze prepared earlier and finish under the broiler for about 1 to 2 minutes. Serve on heated plates with some of the beurre blanc poured around the fish. Serves 4.

Although you will lose some of the smoky overtones to the salmon, a preheated ridged grill pan could be used in place of a charcoal or gas grill. To mince ginger, peel and then thinly slice a knob of ginger. Stack the slices and cut lengthwise into thin strips. Gather the strips together and cut into very small dice.

Chapter 7

The Smoker

he discovery of smoking foods to preserve them is lost in prehistory. Up until the early 1800s, when reliable refrigeration (insulated boxes cooled with ice) and canning methods were developed, the historic methods of food preservation—drying, smoking, salting, and pickling—had remained popular for centuries.

Today most smoking is done primarily because we like the flavor of the smoked food, not because we wish to preserve it for an extended period. To that end smoked foods abound in our supermarkets, from fish to sausages to hams.

It is an easy task to smoke our own foods. Fish, in fact, is far and away the simplest food to smoke in a home smoker. The quickest way to begin smoking at home is to buy an electric smoker, which may be purchased from numerous outdoor catalogs and stores. One advantage electric smokers have over homemade smokers is more precise temperature control, which allows you to cold smoke as well as to smoke-cook foods. Charcoal smokers are also available from the same sources.

Cold smoking (below 100°F) is used to preserve foods for long-term storage without refrigeration. For example, brined fish that are cold smoked for one week will keep approximately one year.

Hot smoking (between 170°F and 250°F), on the other hand, is more common and both smokes and cooks the food for more immediate consumption. For extra smoky flavor, foods are sometimes cold smoked for a length of time, then finished with hot smoke. Fish that has been properly cured and hot smoked should last about a week to ten days under refrigeration.

Smoked fish (like most smoked foods) do not freeze extremely well. If you must freeze them, the dryer smoked fish freeze better than the moist ones, which develop a mushy texture after freezing.

Homemade smokers can be constructed from diverse materials. Primitive smokers constructed from sticks can be used to smoke fish and meats over a backcountry campfire. (See "How to Make a Backcountry Stick Smoker" on p. 167.) More elaborate smokers are constructed from wood, stone, or masonry. Fifty-gallon steel drums, old refrigerators, and even cardboard boxes can be converted into smokers. My smoker is an old stainless steel army field kitchen, which I have converted to use with charcoal. A number of books are available at bookstores and libraries that give detailed instructions for building your own smoker.

The best woods for smoking are hardwoods. Hickory, apple, mesquite, and alder (available as chips, chunks, or sawdust) are sold in many supermarkets and hardware stores in small bags. Hickory and apple are probably the two most popular woods to smoke with, but mesquite is also very popular, especially in the Southwest. Alder is a favored wood for smoking salmon in the Pacific Northwest. Less easy to come by is one of my favorites, maple. In some parts of the country dry corncobs are used with excellent results. To get maximum smoke, the chips or chunks are usually soaked in water before using.

Fish and meats to be smoked are brined (cured) first. The most basic brine is a simple 80 percent solution of salt and water, approximately 3 cups of kosher or pickling salt to a gallon of water. An easy way to achieve this solution for any amount of brine is to put a fairly fresh, raw, unpeeled potato into a container holding the amount of cold water you need to cover your fish or meat. It will sink to the bottom. Slowly stir in the salt. When you have added enough salt to reach an 80 percent solution, the potato will float.

If you are going to go to the trouble of stoking up your smoker, you might as well add a few extra items. Fish and meats aren't the only things that are delicious smoked. All manner of vegetables are wonderful smoked (no lengthy brining is needed either). Thus this chapter includes a basic recipe for smoked fish along with directions for smoking such varied items as tomatoes, onions, wild mushrooms, and peppers, plus recipes for their use.

How to Make a Backcountry Stick Smoker

When the fishing has been good on an extended camping trip, it is sometimes desirable to smoke fish to add a little variety to our menu. Here are directions for constructing a primitive smoker out of materials close at hand.

Wilderness Materials List

Uprights: 4 fairly straight branches, 5 feet long by 1 to 1½ inches thick, sharpened on one end

Crosspieces: 4 fairly straight branches about 2 feet by ¾ inch thick

For the rack: fairly straight branches about ½ to ¾ inch thick and long enough to reach across the crosspieces, as needed

Cordage or wire as needed to lash crosspieces

Directions

Drive the pointed end of the uprights into the ground around a small campfire forming a square approximately 2 feet by 2 feet. Use the cordage or wire to lash the 4 crosspieces about 1 foot below the tops of the uprights to form a square. These should be about 3 to 4 feet above the ground. Lay the rack pieces across the crosspieces.

Using the Smoker

The campfire may be made on the ground or in a pit directly beneath the rack of the smoker. WARNING: Make sure your fire is built on mineral soil. Non-mineral soil, which is found in much of Minnesota's Superior National Forest and the BWCAW, is not only flammable, but once kindled, a fire can smolder underground undetected only to pop up some distance away. In addition, fires in the BWCAW are allowed only in U.S. Forest Service fire grates.

The fire should be small and after it is burning well it should be fueled with green hardwood. If you are in an area where the trees consist mostly of conifers, birch, and poplar, choose the birch but be sure to remove the bark to avoid sooting up your smoked food.

Lay or hang the food to be smoked on the rack. Cover the rack with a tarp, plastic sheet, pine boughs, or anything that will help to contain the smoke. If there is a breeze you might need to place the food closer to the fire.

Note: Fish smoked in remote areas without any kind of refrigeration should be consumed on the same day they are smoked. In bear country it would be a good idea to burn the leftovers from the fish, along with the sticks from the smoker.

Applewood-Smoked Peppered Lake Trout or Salmon

This is an excellent all-purpose brine for fish to be smoked. Fish with a modicum of fat in the flesh smoke up the most succulent and flavorful, hence lake trout, stream trout, salmon, whitefish, herring, and ciscoes are much favored for smoking. Fish that are very lean, such as walleye, northern pike, bass, sunfish, and crappies may also be smoked if they are basted from time to time during the smoking process with vegetable oil, which not only keeps them from drying out, but enhances their flavor.

Brining times vary according to the size of the fish and the way it has been prepared. Whole fish take much longer to brine than fillets. Fillets with the skin left on take longer to brine than ones that are skinless. Lean fish take less time to brine than oily fish. So the whole issue of brining times is largely a guessing game.

Experimentation is the best way to find the amount of brining time that will season your smoked fish to your liking. I have found that if I brine whole skin-on salmon fillets weighing about 3 to 4 pounds (3/4- to 1-inch thick) for 4 to 5 hours under refrigeration I achieve the flavor I like. As a general rule then, we can figure that a 1- to 2-pound fish should be brined for 2 to 3 hours, a 2- to 3-pound fish for 3 to 4 hours, and so on.

> 1 gallon cold tap water
> 3 cups kosher or pickling salt
> 1 cup lemon juice
> 1 cup packed brown sugar
> ⅓ to ½ cup dried dill weed (optional—excellent with salmon)
> ⅓ cup minced fresh garlic

Combine brine ingredients, stirring well until salt and sugar are dissolved. Submerge fish in brine and place a plate or other nonreactive object on top of the fish to keep them submerged. Brine under refrigeration for 30 minutes to overnight, depending on the species of fish, its weight, and how it has been prepared for smoking.

Remove from brine and rinse fish with cold water. Place on rack in sheet pan and dry uncovered in the refrigerator overnight or dry for 30 minutes or so using a fan.

When fish surface is dry and the shiny surface called the "pellicle" has formed, it is time to add any additional flavors. One of my favorites is to sprinkle the fish lightly with brown sugar and rub it in with my hand. Then I grind coarse black pepper over the brown sugar. Other suggested flavorings include maple syrup (highly recommended), Cajun seasoning, or chopped fresh dill weed, to name a few.

If you're using a smoker you have purchased, follow the manufacturer's instructions for hot smoking using apple wood for 2½ to 3½ hours or until fish is cooked through and nicely browned from the smoke. If any problem arises during smoking and the fish do not finish cooking, remove them from the smoker and finish cooking them in a 250°F oven. Alder, hickory, or other hardwood chips may also be used, either alone or in combination. If you are using a homemade smoker, the smoking temperature should be approximately 200°F to 250°F. The amount of smoking time is largely one of personal taste and depends mostly on whether you like your smoked fish moist or dry.

Serve the smoked fish as an appetizer with thinly sliced onions, Chive Horseradish Sauce (p. 223), and thin slices of good rye bread or crackers.

Northwoods Smoked Trout Benedict

Here is a superb breakfast or brunch dish using smoked fish. If you've just won the lottery, you can top the dish with caviar instead of the wild rice. This would be excellent served with a broiled tomato half and buttered asparagus spears if the season were right.

Per person:
1 English muffin, split and toasted
2 to 3 washed and dried fresh spinach leaves
1 to 2 ounces smoked trout, salmon, or other fish, home smoked or from the store
1 egg, poached
2 ounces Chive Hollandaise Sauce (p. 233)
1 tablespoon cooked wild rice to garnish (optional)

Top one half of the English muffin with 2 or 3 spinach leaves and then smoked trout, either a single piece approximately the size of the muffin or broken chunks. Place a hot poached egg on top of the trout and spoon Chive-Hollandaise Sauce over the top. Sprinkle with cooked wild rice. Butter the other half of the English muffin and serve with the Benedict. Serves 1.

Eggs may be poached up to a day ahead. Poach the eggs as usual and place in a pan of cold water. Refrigerate the poached eggs in the water. To reheat gently drop the already poached eggs into a pan of barely simmering water for about a minute or until heated through.

Smoked Fish Potato Cakes

Make these smoked fish cakes with any leftover mashed potatoes. I like these for breakfast served alongside a couple of eggs prepared any style.

> 12 ounces smoked fish, bones removed and flaked
> ⅓ cup minced onions
> 2 cups cold mashed potatoes
> 3 tablespoons chopped parsley
> 1 egg beaten
> Salt and freshly ground black pepper to taste
> Vegetable oil, as needed

In a large bowl combine all ingredients and mix well. With floured hands, shape into four ¾-inch thick round cakes. Cover the bottom of a 10-inch or 12-inch skillet (a griddle may also be used) set over medium heat with just enough vegetable oil to cover the bottom. Dust the cakes with flour and fry in hot oil until browned on both sides and hot throughout. Makes 4 large cakes.

Smoked Tomato Puree

This wonderful smoked tomato puree is a versatile base for making everything from pastas to sauces. Season some of the puree with a little salt, a pinch of sugar, and some dried oregano for a unique pizza sauce.

> 3 pounds tomatoes, halved
> Vegetable oil
> 1 head garlic, separated into cloves and peeled (optional)
> 4 to 6 fresh thyme sprigs (optional)

Place tomato halves in a large bowl with the garlic and thyme if you decide to use them. Toss with vegetable oil to coat lightly. Turn out onto a shallow-sided sheet pan and turn the tomatoes so the cut side is up. Place in smoker and smoke for 2 to 3 hours or until tomatoes are cooked through. Remove from smoker and let cool.

Leaving the juices behind, place the tomatoes, garlic (optional), and thyme into a food processor fitted with a metal blade and puree (in batches if necessary). Put through a strainer to remove seeds and skin. The remaining watery juices may be strained and used to add delicious smoked flavor to soups or sauces. *Puree and remaining juices may be prepared ahead and refrigerated for a week or frozen for up to 6 months.*

Smoked Tomato Vinaigrette

Use this mildly spicy, smoky vinaigrette on mixed greens or as a sauce for grilled or roasted fish.

> 2 cloves roasted garlic
> 2 shallots, minced
> 1 dried ancho chile
> 1½ cups Smoked Tomato Puree
> 2 tablespoons balsamic vinegar
> ½ cup vegetable oil
> ½ cup extra-virgin olive oil
> 2 to 4 tablespoons maple syrup (or to taste)
> Salt and freshly ground black pepper to taste

Remove the seeds and stem of the ancho chile and soak it in hot tap water for 30 minutes or until softened. Drain and discard soaking water. Place soaked chile in blender along with the remaining ingredients except salt and pepper. Blend until emulsified. Season to taste with salt, pepper, and additional maple syrup, if desired. May be made up to 2 weeks ahead and refrigerated. Makes about 2½ cups.

Smoked Tomato-Parmesan Linguine

This linguine tossed with a creamy smoke-scented tomato sauce has been a favorite vegetarian entrée for several years in the dining room at Gunflint Lodge.

> 2 tablespoons olive oil
> 1 tablespoon minced garlic
> ½ cup julienned red onions
> Pinch of crushed red pepper flakes (optional)
> 1 fresh firm ripe tomato, seeded and cut into ¼-inch dice
> 2 ounces (¼ cup) smoked tomato puree
> 3 to 4 tablespoons chopped fresh basil (or to taste)
> 1 teaspoon salt
> Pinch sugar
> 1 to 2 ounces heavy cream
> 4 ounces dry linguine, cooked al dente
> ¼ cup freshly grated Parmesan cheese for topping

In a 10-inch skillet set over medium-low heat, sauté the garlic, onions, and red pepper flakes (if you decide to use them) in the olive oil until the onions are transparent. Add the tomatoes, smoked tomato puree, basil, salt, pepper, sugar, and cream. Add the pasta and toss together until everything is hot. Turn out onto a heated plate or pasta bowl and top with the Parmesan cheese. Serves 2 as a first course or 1 as an entrée.

Creamy Smoke-Roasted Onion Soup with Parmesan Cheese

This earthy smoky soup is definitely not your father's French onion soup. Serve this with some crusty bread or bake it topped with a crisp garlic crouton and Swiss cheese.

    4 cups chicken or beef stock, homemade or low-sodium canned
    ¼ teaspoon minced fresh garlic
    6 tablespoons butter
    6 tablespoons flour
    1 cup smoke-roasted onion puree or more to taste (recipe below)
    ¼ cup heavy cream
    Salt and freshly ground black pepper to taste
    Freshly grated Parmesan

In a 2-quart saucepan set over medium heat, bring the chicken or beef stock and garlic to a simmer. In a small saucepan set over medium-low heat, make a roux by melting the butter and whisking in the flour. Whisk and cook for a minute or so without browning to remove the raw flour taste, then remove from heat and let cool. Whisk the cooled roux into the simmering stock and bring to a boil, whisking constantly. The soup should have the consistency of a thin white sauce. Reduce if too thin or add additional stock or water if too thick. Strain into another saucepan and stir in the roasted onion puree. Simmer for 20 minutes. Stir in the heavy cream. Season to taste with salt and pepper. *May be made up to 3 days ahead and refrigerated covered or frozen for up to 6 months.*

Smoke-Roasted Onion Puree

    2 pounds large yellow onions
    Vegetable oil as needed

Peel and halve large onions and place in a large bowl. Toss with vegetable oil to coat lightly. Place cut side down on a large sheet pan, then place in smoker and smoke roast for about 3 hours at 200°F to 250°F. If necessary, onions may finish roasting in a 300°F oven until tender. Puree in batches in a food processor. *May be made ahead and refrigerated for a week or frozen for up to 6 months.*

Smoked Yellow Peppers

These are used to make the Smoked Yellow Pepper Remoulade on p. 226.

Rub whole yellow peppers with olive oil and lay on rack in smoker. Follow the manufacturer's instructions for hot smoking using any hardwood chips or sawdust. If you are using a home-made smoker, the smoking temperature should be approximately 200°F to 250°F. Smoke for 2 to 3 hours until peppers are somewhat soft and the skin is wrinkled. Remove from smoker and cool. Remove skin and seeds. *May be prepared up to a week ahead and refrigerated until needed or they may be wrapped closely in plastic wrap and frozen for up to 6 months.*

Cream of Smoked Wild Forest Mushroom Soup

Try this creamy soup with its wonderful smoky flavors once and you'll want to make it again and again. This soup freezes well. Voted best soup at the first North Shore "Souper Bowl."

1 ½ pounds fresh wild mushrooms, such as shiitakes, chanterelles, morels, or porcini, smoked over apple wood or hickory (see next page)
1 medium onion, chopped
1 small leek, white and yellow part only, chopped
½ teaspoon minced garlic
8 tablespoons butter
8 tablespoons flour
6 cups chicken stock, homemade or low-sodium canned (see next page)
½ cup half-and-half
½ cup heavy cream
Salt and freshly ground black pepper to taste

Mushrooms may be smoked in any smoker. Place the fresh wild mushrooms in a shallow pan, such as a cake pan. Toss the mushrooms with a little vegetable oil to coat them lightly and place in smoker. Hot smoke mushrooms until soft throughout and nicely browned from the smoke. Remove from smoker and cool.

Set aside about ¼ of the mushrooms to be sliced and added later to the soup. In a food processor with a metal blade, finely chop the remaining mushrooms. Reserve the juices from the smoked mushrooms to add to the soup with the chicken broth.

To make the soup, heat a heavy 4-quart stockpot or Dutch oven over very low heat and melt the butter. Add the onions, leeks, and garlic. Cover and cook until onions are translucent and tender, but not browned. Stir in the flour; cook without browning for 2 minutes. Whisk in the stock and the reserved wild mushroom liquid. Increase heat to medium and cook, whisking constantly, until soup thickens and comes to a boil. Reduce heat to low and add the chopped smoked mushrooms. Simmer, stirring frequently, for 20 minutes. Strain soup, pushing down hard on the solids to extract as much of the liquid as possible. Discard the solids. Return soup to pan and stir in the half-

and-half and heavy cream. Slice and add the reserved mushrooms. Season to taste with salt and freshly ground black pepper. Bring soup back to a simmer and serve. Makes about 9 to 10 cups.

White mushrooms may replace up to half of the wild mushrooms. All of the chicken stock may be replaced with an equal amount of water seasoned to taste with a high quality chicken base. To use dry wild mushrooms, soak 2 ounces of them in hot water to cover for 30 minutes. Drain, reserving liquid for soup, and toss together with 1 pound fresh white mushrooms. Smoke as directed on page 176 and prepare soup as directed.

Chapter 8

Accompaniments

he main entrée may be the star attraction on the plate, but to really shine, the star needs a costar or two. You will find a varied selection of costars in this chapter.

Nearly everybody likes mashed potatoes and they go as well with fish as they do with meat. An acquaintance once told me why he disliked fish: "What good is fish," he groused, "if you can't make gravy from it?" Granted we will have no "gravy" from the fish to spoon over our mashers, but with ten different ways to mash them, I doubt we will miss the gravy.

Tradition decrees fried potatoes with onions and pork and beans as shore lunch accompaniments. I suggest a couple of variations that will enliven your next shore lunch or fish fry—a tangy potato salad with a Parmesan peppercorn dressing and spicy beans with the smoky heat of chipotle chiles.

In addition to a couple of wild rice pilaf recipes is a recipe for risotto, the famous rice dish of Italy. It is a fine accompaniment to fish and can be varied in numerous ways. Also for your dining pleasure I have included a pair of my favorite vegetable dishes to serve with fish.

Basic Risotto

Here is a basic recipe for risotto that lends itself to endless variations. Be sure to use Arborio rice; regular rice will not absorb the necessary amount of liquid without turning into mush.

> 4½ cups light chicken broth, homemade or low-sodium canned
> 1½ tablespoons butter
> 1½ cups Arborio rice
> 1 small onion, diced (about ½ cup)
> ¾ cup dry white wine
> 1 tablespoon butter
> ½ cup freshly grated Parmesan cheese
> Salt and freshly ground black pepper to taste

Heat the chicken stock to a boil; reduce heat to a simmer. In a medium heavy-gauge saucepan set over medium-high heat, melt the butter and stir in the rice. Stir the rice for a minute or two without browning. Add the onions and stir constantly until the onions are translucent, another minute or two. Add the wine and cook until almost all of the liquid has disappeared, about a minute. Add just enough hot broth to cover the rice, adjusting the heat so that bubbles just break the surface. Cook, stirring occasionally, until the stock is absorbed by the rice. Continue to add more broth until rice is al dente, which will take about 20 minutes. Bite into a grain of the rice and you should see a small white pin dot in the center. Add the butter and the cheese and stir to incorporate. Serve immediately. Serves 6.

Optional additions:

> Stir in one or more of the following with the butter and cheese:
> Sliced cooked asparagus
> Roasted, braised, or blanched fennel, chopped
> Cooked broccoli, chopped
> Basil pesto
> Roasted red peppers cut into medium dice
> Sautéed sliced wild or domestic mushrooms
> Diced cooked butternut squash

To make ahead: After half of the stock (along with flavoring, such as saffron) has been added and absorbed, immediately spread the risotto out on a plate or shallow pan to cool. Cover and refrigerate until ready to use. To finish cooking the risotto, put the desired amount of cold risotto in a skillet set over medium-high heat, adding simmering stock as necessary to complete cooking the risotto. Stir in butter and cheese and any of the optional additions and serve.

Mashed Potatoes Ten Different Ways

As comfort foods go, mashed potatoes rank near the top. Mashed potatoes and fish are so superb together that I often serve fish right on top of them. Here is a basic recipe for mashed potatoes followed by nine savory variations.

Basic Mashed Potatoes

> 2½ pounds gold or red potatoes, peeled and halved
> 4 quarts of cold water seasoned with 1 tablespoon salt
> 2 to 4 tablespoons soft butter
> Milk, buttermilk, buttermilk or milk plus cream, half-and-half, or cream as
>   needed, heated
> Salt and freshly ground black pepper to taste

Add the potatoes to the salted water. Bring to a boil over high heat and cook until a fork goes through the potatoes easily. Drain and return to saucepan. Shake the pan with the potatoes over medium-high heat to evaporate remaining moisture. Place potatoes into a warm bowl and mash, either by hand or with a mixer, adding the butter to taste and enough of the hot milk as needed to mash to desired consistency. Season to taste with salt and pepper. Serves 6.

Each of the following recipes is based in part on the basic recipe above. In each recipe, the potatoes are to be cooked, drained, and dried as directed above. Add and substitute ingredients as directed.

Fennel Mashed Potatoes

Pair fennel mashed potatoes with fish for a match made in heaven. A different version of fennel mashed potatoes using braised fennel is described in the Seared Bass recipe on p. 136.

Add 3 large cloves of garlic, peeled and halved, to cook along with the potatoes.

Substitute the following prepared mixture for the milk:

> 2 bulbs fennel
> ½ cup heavy cream

While the potatoes and garlic are cooking, trim stalks flush with fennel bulbs and cut a thin slice off the base. Cut the bulb lengthwise into quarters and remove and discard the cores. Chop coarsely and place with the cream in a small saucepan set over medium-low heat. Cover and cook at a low simmer until fennel is very soft, about 12 to 15 minutes. Puree fennel and cream in a food processor fitted with a metal blade.

Mash potatoes and garlic with the fennel puree together with the greater amount of butter (4 tablespoons) and additional cream as needed for consistency. Season to taste with salt and pepper.

Roasted Garlic Mashed Potatoes

Add roasted garlic puree (procedure below) to taste to Basic Mashed Potatoes when adding the milk and butter. You will need about 1 head of roasted garlic pureed for this recipe.

Roasted Garlic Puree

Remove as much of the papery outer layer as you can from whole heads of garlic and cut off the top third of each head. Discard the tops or save for another use such as flavoring a stock. Or you can peel and chop the top portions of the cloves, cover with a little olive oil in a small dish, and store in your refrigerator for up to a week and use as needed. To roast the garlic, brush the cut surface of each garlic head with olive oil and wrap tightly in aluminum foil. Roast in a 350°F oven for about one hour or until garlic is soft. Remove from oven and let cool. Squeeze the garlic cloves from the heads and puree them while still warm in a food processor with a metal blade or in a blender. Refrigerate until needed. Leftover roasted garlic puree keeps well in the refrigerator. It may also be frozen for a month or so.

Garlic and Sour Cream Mashed Potatoes

My general rule for these potatoes is to add one whole peeled clove of garlic per potato. Add more or fewer garlic cloves to adjust the intensity of the garlic to your preferences. These can be made ahead and reheated more successfully than most mashed potatoes. Reheat covered in the oven or in the microwave. For a guilt-free version, use lowfat or nonfat sour cream and omit the butter.

Add 6 to 8 large cloves of garlic, peeled and halved, to cook along with the potatoes. Mash potatoes and garlic with butter to taste, substituting full fat, light, or nonfat sour cream for the milk as needed for proper consistency. Season to taste with salt and pepper.

Horseradish Mashed Potatoes

Add 6 to 8 large cloves of garlic, peeled and halved, to cook along with the potatoes.

Substitute the following prepared mixture for the milk:

> 1 cup cream
> 1 shallot, minced
> 4 to 8 tablespoons prepared horseradish to taste

While the potatoes and garlic are cooking, combine the cream with the minced shallot and prepared horseradish to taste in a small saucepan. Bring to a boil and reduce heat. Simmer slowly for 3 to 4 minutes.

Mash potatoes and garlic, adding the horseradish mixture as needed for proper consistency along with butter to taste. If necessary, add additional cream or milk. Season to taste with salt and pepper.

Parmesan Mashed Potatoes

Other cheeses may be substituted for the Parmesan. Try Gruyère, Swiss, cheddar, or Romano. Soft goat cheese is an excellent addition to both the Basic Mashed Potatoes and the Roasted Garlic Mashed Potatoes. Add 3 to 6 large cloves of garlic, peeled and halved, to cook along with the potatoes (optional). Mash potatoes and garlic, if you decide to use it, adding 2 ounces (about ½ cup) of freshly grated Parmesan cheese along with butter to taste and milk as needed for consistency. Season to taste with salt and pepper.

Herb Mashed Potatoes

Add about ⅓ cup chopped fresh basil or other fresh herb or herb combination to Basic Mashed Potatoes when adding the milk and butter. In place of the fresh herbs, you can add about ½ cup of basil pesto sauce before adding the milk, then adding milk as needed for consistency.

Roasted Wild Mushroom Mashed Potatoes

Add 6 large cloves of garlic, peeled and halved, to cook along with the potatoes.

> 1 pound coarsely chopped, fresh, wild mushrooms such as shiitake (stems removed), chanterelle, oyster, morel, or a combination
> ¼ cup olive oil
> Salt and freshly ground black pepper to taste

While the potatoes are cooking, place the mushrooms in a roasting dish, coat with the olive oil and season lightly with salt and pepper. Cover the dish with aluminum foil and roast in a 350°F oven until the mushrooms are tender (about 20 to 30 minutes).

Scrape the roasted mushrooms and olive oil into the potatoes and garlic, adding butter to taste and cream as needed. Incorporate all ingredients with a potato masher, leaving the mixture partially chunky. Season to taste with salt and pepper. A couple of tablespoons of chopped parsley may also be added to the potatoes if desired.

Mashed Potatoes with Cabbage and Green Onions (Colcannon)

This is Irish comfort food and one of my favorite ways to mash potatoes. Reduce potatoes to 2 pounds and cook as directed in Basic Mashed Potatoes recipe.

> 1 small head of cabbage (about 1 pound), cored and cut into 1-inch
>   pieces
> 2 bunches green onions, white part only, sliced (reserve tops for garnish)

While the potatoes are cooking, use the larger amount of butter (4 tablespoons) called for in the recipe and melt it in a large skillet set over medium-low heat. Add the chopped cabbage, the sliced green onions, and a tablespoon or so of water. Cover the pan and sweat the vegetables until very tender, about 30 minutes or so, stirring from time to time. By the time the cabbage mixture is cooked, the water should be evaporated. If any moisture remains, remove the cabbage and green onions with a slotted spoon and boil until water evaporates.

Mash cabbage mixture and butter together with the potatoes, adding milk as needed and additional butter if desired. Top potatoes with some thinly sliced reserved green onion tops for garnish if desired.

Celeriac Mashed Potatoes

Celeriac is a root vegetable with the strong taste of celery and the texture of a turnip. It forms a wonderful partnership with potatoes.

Substitute the following prepared mixture for the milk:
2 knobs of celeriac
½ cup cream
Large pinch of salt

Prepare the celeriac by peeling off the fibrous skin, cutting off any stalks and root ends. Cut into ½-inch cubes and combine with the cream and a large pinch of salt in a small saucepan set over medium-low heat. Cover and cook for 20 to 30 minutes or until the celeriac is very soft. Puree in food processor fitted with a metal blade.

Mash the celeriac puree and cooked drained potatoes together with butter to taste and additional cream as needed for consistency. Season to taste with salt and pepper.

Northwoods Wild Rice Pilaf

For centuries wild rice was harvested every fall by Native Americans. Wild rice supplied about 25 percent of their diet and numerous tribal wars were fought for control of the shallow waters where the wild rice grew. To harvest the rice, one person pushed a canoe through the beds with a long pole, while another sat in the bottom of the canoe and bent the tall wild rice plants over the canoe, beating the stalks gently with wooden flails to knock the ripe kernels off into the bottom of the canoe. About four-fifths of the rice fell back into the water, providing seed for future crops.

Minnesota ranks as one of the top producers of this distinctive native grass seed. For many years the price of wild rice fluctuated wildly, depending on the harvest. When a wild rice plant was developed that did not shed its grain when ripe, a new industry was born—the growing of wild rice in paddies. While, like the commercial tomato, this was not a great gastronomic leap forward, the price has remained fairly stable since its introduction.

Wild rice harvested in the traditional manner from lakes and rivers is also available and even though it costs a little more, I prefer it over the paddy rice. Minnesota-grown wild rice must state on the package whether it is paddy grown or not.

> 1 cup wild rice, cooked according to package directions in homemade or low-sodium canned chicken broth
> 4 tablespoons butter
> ¼ teaspoon minced garlic (optional)
> 1 medium onion, finely chopped
> 1 small green pepper, finely chopped
> ½ red pepper, finely chopped (optional)
> 4 ounces fresh mushrooms, sliced
> 2 tablespoons chopped parsley
> Salt and freshly ground black pepper to taste

In a large skillet melt the butter over medium heat. Add the optional garlic, onions, green and red peppers, and mushrooms and sauté until the vegetables are soft. Toss vegetable mixture with the cooked wild rice and the chopped parsley. Season to taste with salt and pepper. Serves 6 to 8 as a side dish.

➤🐟 Crisp crumbled bacon is a nice addition, as are canned water chestnuts, drained and coarsely chopped.

Oriental Wild Rice and Spinach Pilaf

This colorful side dish goes well with many fish dishes, but it goes especially well with the richness of salmon and trout.

⅔ cup wild rice, cooked according to package directions in homemade or low-sodium canned chicken broth
3 tablespoons butter
½ medium onion, diced
4 ounces fresh white mushroom caps or shiitakes, thinly sliced
½ red pepper, minced
1 10-ounce package frozen spinach
3 to 4 ounces canned water chestnuts, drained and coarsely chopped
Soy sauce and freshly ground black pepper to taste

Sauté the onions, mushrooms, and red pepper in the butter in a skillet set over medium heat until the onions are transparent. At the same time, cook the spinach according to package directions and let cool until it can be handled. Squeeze as much water as possible out of the spinach and chop it.

In a large bowl, combine the cooked wild rice, the vegetable mixture, the chopped spinach, and the chopped chestnuts if you decide to use them, tossing to combine well. Season with soy sauce and pepper to taste. Scrape into a shallow casserole dish and cover. *May be made up to a day ahead and refrigerated covered.*

Reheat covered in a preheated 350°F oven for 10 to 15 minutes or until hot. You may also reheat the pilaf in a microwave. Serves 6.

➤🐟 You can substitute one of the very small jars of canned chopped pimento for the red pepper if you like. Add the canned pimento to the wild rice with the spinach.

Pepper Parmesan Potato Salad

What's a picnic without potato salad? Or a shore lunch or fish fry for that matter? Here's a nice alternative to fried potatoes.

> 1½ pounds red or Yukon Gold potatoes, cooked, peeled, and cut into
>   ½- to ¾-inch dice
> ½ cup onions, finely chopped
> ¾ cup celery, finely chopped
> 1½ to 2 teaspoons minced, seeded jalapeño peppers, more to taste
>   (optional)
> 3 hard-boiled eggs, coarsely chopped
> 2 tablespoons sliced Kalamata or Niçoise olives (optional)
> 1½ cups Buttermilk Peppercorn Romano Dressing (recipe on p. 191)
> 2 to 3 tablespoons Dijon mustard (or to taste)
> 2 teaspoons sugar (or to taste)
> ¾ to 1 teaspoon kosher salt (or to taste)
> Freshly ground black pepper
> 1 to 2 additional hard-boiled eggs, sliced for garnish
> Chopped parsley or parsley sprigs for garnish

Combine diced potatoes with onions, celery, jalapeños, chopped hard-boiled eggs, and optional olives. Combine dressing, Dijon mustard, and sugar and toss with potato mixture. Taste for seasoning and add salt and pepper to taste along with additional sugar if desired. Scrape into serving dish and garnish with hard-boiled egg slices and parsley. Refrigerate for at least 2 hours to combine flavors. *May be made up to two days ahead and refrigerated until ready to serve.* Makes about 5 cups serving 8 to 10.

Optional additions and substitutions:

> Sliced radishes
> Sliced green olives
> Chopped sweet pickles
> Crumbled crisp bacon
> Chopped dill pickles
> Pickled asparagus

For best results, cook whole medium-sized potatoes in the skins and peel them as soon as you can handle them. An easier alternative is to leave the skins on the potatoes and either slice or dice them.

Buttermilk Peppercorn Romano Dressing

This is great on greens and baked potatoes as well.

1 cup mayonnaise
1 tablespoon finely minced onions
1 dash hot pepper sauce
⅛ teaspoon Lea and Perrins Worcestershire sauce
⅛ teaspoon balsamic vinegar
¾ teaspoon fresh lemon juice (or to taste)
5 tablespoons buttermilk, plus more as needed to thin dressing
⅛ teaspoon salt (more to taste)
2 tablespoons finely grated Romano cheese
Several grinds coarse black pepper to taste

Combine all ingredients and whisk until well mixed. Store in the refrigerator until needed. Makes about 1½ cups of dressing.

Smoky Chile BBQ Beans

These spicy smoky beans are a perfect accompaniment for a fish fry or shore lunch. Beans have been called "the tartar sauce of the North."

    1 cup navy beans
    4 cups cold water
    3 slices smoked bacon, cut into ¼-inch dice
    1 cup finely diced onion
    ½ cup barbecue sauce, your favorite brand or homemade
    1 to 3 teaspoons finely chopped chipotles *en adobo* (canned smoked
        jalapeño chiles) (or to taste)
    2 tablespoons brown sugar, packed
    1 tablespoon molasses or 2 tablespoons maple syrup (or to taste)
    1 tablespoon ancho chile powder (optional)
    ½ teaspoon salt (more to taste)
    Freshly ground black pepper to taste
    ½ to 1 cup water (or more as needed)

Soak navy beans overnight. (Or use the quick soak method: place the beans in a heavy bottomed 2-quart saucepan and add 4 cups of cold water. Bring to a boil. Boil for 5 minutes, then cover, remove from heat, and let sit for one hour.) Whichever method you use, drain and discard the soaking water.

After soaking, cover the beans with 4 cups of fresh cold water. Bring to a boil, then reduce heat and cook uncovered at a simmer until beans are tender but not mushy, 1 hour or more. Drain and discard remaining cooking liquid.

Mix remaining ingredients into drained beans, adding enough water to come just to the top of the beans. Bring to a boil, then reduce heat to low and simmer for about 1½ to 2 hours, adding water as necessary if beans begin to dry out. Stir the beans as little as possible while cooking to avoid mushing them up. Taste for seasoning and add additional salt and pepper to taste. When finished cooking, the beans will be tender and creamy inside and the liquid will be thickened. *Beans may be refrigerated for up to 1 week or frozen for up to 6 months.* Makes about 4 cups or 6 to 8 servings.

The beans may also be baked in the oven if desired. After the cooking liquid has been drained, place the beans and the remaining ingredients in a bean pot and bake, covered, in a preheated 250°F oven for 4 to 5 hours or until the liquid has thickened.

Chipotles are smoked jalapeños. Chipotles *en adobo* are canned smoked jalapeños in a tangy sauce. They are fiery hot. If your hands are very sensitive, use protective gloves when handling them. Leftover chipotles *en adobo* may be frozen for future use.

Butter-Braised Cucumbers with Dill

Here is a light and tasty accompaniment that goes well with fish.

> 6 cucumbers
> 4½ tablespoons butter
> Salt and freshly ground black pepper to taste
> 1 tablespoon chopped fresh dill or 1 teaspoon dried dill weed

Peel cucumbers, cut in half lengthwise, and scoop out the seeds with a small spoon. Cut each half in half again lengthwise and cut into 2-inch lengths. Bring a pan of salted water to a boil and cook cucumber pieces for 3 to 5 minutes or until almost tender. Drain. *May be made up to 6 hours ahead, then covered and refrigerated.*

To cook, melt butter in a large skillet. Add the cucumbers and sauté for 3 to 4 minutes or until heated through and just tender. Do not overcook or they will be bitter. Remove from heat and season to taste with salt and pepper. Serves 6.

Spinach-Stuffed Tomatoes Gratinée

These tomatoes with their green spinach stuffing flecked with Swiss cheese are a colorful and delicious side dish.

4 firm ripe tomatoes
2 tablespoons minced onions
4 ounces fresh white mushrooms, sliced
Drops of fresh lemon juice
2 tablespoons butter
1 10-ounce package fresh spinach
½ teaspoon salt
Freshly ground black pepper to taste
½ cup sour cream
2 to 3 tablespoons freshly grated Parmesan cheese
¼ cup shredded Swiss cheese
Additional Parmesan cheese, as needed

Cut off the top third of each tomato and hollow out the insides. Lightly sprinkle the insides of the tomatoes with salt and place cut side down on paper towels to drain for 15 minutes.

Sort the spinach, removing any blemished leaves and the coarse stems. Plunge leaves up and down in cold water, shake lightly, and place in a large cook pot set over medium heat. Cover and steam in the water that is clinging to the leaves for 3 to 5 minutes or until wilted. Do not overcook; the leaves should still be bright green. Drain cooked spinach in a colander, pressing with a large spoon to remove excess water. Turn spinach out onto a cutting board and chop coarsely.

Meanwhile in a 10-inch skillet set over medium-high heat, melt the butter and when the foaming subsides, add the mushrooms. Sprinkle with drops of fresh lemon juice and cook, tossing and stirring until the mushrooms are cooked through but not browned. Reduce heat to medium low and add the onions. Cook the onions with the mushrooms until the onions are transparent. Add the chopped spinach and season with salt and pepper. Heat for 5 minutes, stirring occasionally.

In a large bowl, combine the sour cream, Parmesan cheese, and Swiss cheese. Scrape the spinach mixture into the sour cream mixture and stir to combine well. Fill the tomatoes with the stuffing, mounding it slightly, and sprinkle the top of the stuffing with additional Parmesan cheese. *May be made up to 4 hours ahead and refrigerated, covered.*

To bake, preheat oven to 350°F. Bake the tomatoes for 20 to 30 minutes or until heated through. Serve immediately. Serves 4.

Gene's Chipotle Salsa

This salsa recipe is from Gene Buchholz, longtime *sous*-chef at Gunflint Lodge. It adds a cool smoky heat to fish.

> 1½ cups fresh tomatoes, seeded and diced
> ¼ cup yellow onions, finely diced
> 2 tablespoons fresh lime juice
> 1 to 3 teaspoons pureed or finely minced chipotles *en adobo,* or to taste
>   (Use chipotles and shake off as much of the *adobo* sauce as you can.)
> 1 teaspoon ground cumin
> 1 tablespoon chopped cilantro
> Salt and sugar to taste

Make the salsa by combining the tomatoes, onions, lime juice, and pureed or minced chipotles *en adobo.* Season to taste with cumin, cilantro, salt, sugar, and additional chipotle puree to taste. Serve at room temperature. *For best results, use within 2 to 3 hours.* Makes about 2 cups.

Chapter 9

Stuffings, Breadings, and Seasonings

tched in my memory is the recollection of a simply stuffed lake trout wrapped in foil and roasted in the coals of a Boundary Waters campfire many years ago. As I recall, the stuffing was cobbled together out of ingredients at hand—some chopped fresh tomatoes I had carefully packed (reconstituted dried tomatoes would have worked just as well) plus chopped fresh onions and a little garlic I sautéed in butter. I tossed my vegetable mixture with crumbled fresh bread and seasoned it with salt and a good amount of black pepper. I still remember the aromas that issued from that foil package as I opened it up. The succulent flesh tasted faintly smoky and the stuffing had been rendered even more delicious by some of the juices of the trout. You will find several savory stuffings to try in this chapter.

It's fun to experiment with different breadings for fried fish. The recipe for Northwoods All-Purpose Breading Mix is a versatile make-ahead breading mix that forms the basis for a multitude of breadings, from the simple fishing guide's shore lunch breading to nut and crumb coatings. The beer batter variation makes not only the finest beer batter on the planet, but also the simplest.

The artful use of seasonings is the soul of flavorful cooking. Thus you will find recipes for some useful seasoning mixtures that will add extra flavor to your fish. Remember that any seasonings you use should complement the flavor of the food, not dominate it.

Summer Herb Stuffing

This herbal stuffing combines the fresh flavors of summer with the delicate essence of freshly caught game fish. Check out the five variations of this multipurpose stuffing listed at the end of the recipe.

> 6 tablespoons butter
> 1½ teaspoons minced garlic
> ¾ cup finely chopped onions
> ¾ cup finely chopped celery
> 3 tablespoons dry white vermouth
> ¼ cup finely chopped green onion tops or chives
> ¼ cup chopped flat leaf (Italian) parsley
> 3 tablespoons chopped fresh basil or 2 tablespoons chopped fresh dill
> 4 cups fresh white bread crumbs
> 4 to 8 tablespoons heavy cream to moisten
> ½ teaspoon of fresh lemon juice (or to taste)
> Salt and freshly ground black pepper to taste

In a skillet set over low heat, sweat the garlic, onions, and celery in butter until onions are translucent. Add dry white vermouth, increase heat, and bring to a boil. Boil for 1 minute. Remove from heat and stir in fresh herbs. Scrape into a bowl and add the bread crumbs. Toss to combine, adding just enough cream to moisten the stuffing. Add fresh lemon juice and season to taste with salt and pepper. Makes enough stuffing for 2½ pounds of fish fillets or a 5- to 6-pound whole dressed fish. *May be made ahead to this point, wrapped closely in plastic wrap, and refrigerated for up to 3 days or frozen for up to 6 months.*

Use a food processor with a metal blade to make the bread crumbs. A 1-pound loaf of French or Italian bread with crusts removed makes about 2 quarts of fresh bread crumbs.

Variations

Summer Herb and Garden Tomato Stuffing:

Add 1 peeled, seeded, and diced firm ripe garden tomato when adding the herbs.

Spinach Stuffing:

Omit the green onion tops, basil, parsley, and the dry white vermouth or wine. After sautéing the garlic, onions, and celery in the butter, add 1 10-ounce package of frozen spinach (or an equal amount of cooked fresh spinach) that has been thawed, squeezed completely dry, and chopped. Increase heat to medium high and cook the spinach mixture, stirring constantly, to evaporate most of the moisture. Scrape into bowl and proceed with recipe.

Bacon Stuffing:

Replace the butter with bacon fat. Omit the basil or dill. Add ¼ cup crumbled crisp bacon with the bread crumbs.

Mushroom Stuffing:

Sauté 4 ounces of coarsely chopped fresh button or wild mushrooms with the onions and celery.

Crab Stuffing:

Add ⅓ cup finely chopped green peppers to the celery and onions. Omit the basil or dill. Add ½ to ¾ cup cooked crabmeat (or lobster meat). Add additional lemon juice to taste. Also add drops of Worcestershire sauce and hot pepper sauce to taste.

See also Green Chile Stuffing (p. 102), Salmon Mousseline (p. 116), Bacon-Hazelnut Stuffing (p. 126), Lobster Stuffing (p. 128), and Fresh Garden Herb Stuffing (p. 132).

How to Stuff a Fish

Whole Fish

Any whole fish may be stuffed, but prime candidates are whole salmon, lake trout, stream trout, and larger walleye, northern pike, and muskellunge. A roasted whole stuffed fish looks impressive and feeds many.

The easiest way to stuff a whole fish is to simply place the stuffing into the cavity of the cleaned fish and truss. However, removing the bones before stuffing is not a difficult job (see "Simple Surgery: Removing Bones from Trout," p. 123) and stuffed boneless fish are easier to serve and eat.

The fish to be stuffed should first be scaled (except for all trout and salmon, which do not need to be scaled since their scales are so small and soft).

Whole stuffed fish should be baked in a preheated 450°F oven for approximately 10 minutes for every inch of thickness of the fish when measured across the thickest part of the back of the fish.

Fillets

Fillets to be stuffed should be both boneless and skinless and there are several ways to get stuffing into a fish fillet. Here are four popular stuffing strategies:

Two-Fillet Method:

This stuffing method requires two fillets of approximately the same size. For individual servings the fillets to be stuffed should be quite small (3 to 4 ounces each). Larger fillets may also be stuffed and cut into individual servings after baking. Fillets from the same side make the nicest presentation, but this is not necessary.

Place one fillet skin side down on a baking sheet or pie tin sprayed with nonstick cooking spray. Season lightly with salt and pepper and spread a mound of stuffing down the middle of the fillet about an inch high and an inch wide extending to within 1 to 1½ inches of each end of the fillet. Take another fillet and with a sharp knife make a slit lengthwise down the middle of the fillet, leaving about ¾ to 1 inch uncut on each end to keep the fillet connected. Lay this split fillet, skin side up or down as looks best, over the stuffing, spreading the cut wide to let the stuffing mound up through the opening. Brush the stuffed fish with butter and season lightly with salt and pepper. Sprinkle only the fish with paprika to allow the stuffing to stand in contrast. Pour white wine, white wine and water, or water around the fish and bake in a preheated 425°F oven until just cooked.

Casserole Method:

Place a layer of fish fillets in a slightly overlapping layer on the bottom of a buttered shallow casserole dish. Spread the stuffing over the fish, then top with another layer of fillets. Brush the top of the fish with butter, season with salt, pepper, and paprika, and bake in a preheated 400°F oven until a skewer goes through the fish with no resistance.

Single-Fillet Roulade Method:

Spread the stuffing on the fillet and roll it up, making a roulade. Use toothpicks to hold the roulades together. Stand the roulades on their sides or lay them down and bake in a preheated 400°F oven until just cooked.

Single-Fillet Folded Method:

Lay each fillet to be stuffed with the skin side up on a buttered baking pan. Lightly score with a sharp knife to prevent curling. Place about 2 heaping tablespoons of the stuffing just below center toward the large end of the fillet and fold the tail end over the stuffing. If necessary, toothpicks may be used to secure the fish. Brush with butter, season with salt and pepper, and sprinkle with paprika if desired. Pour a little white wine or white wine and water around the stuffed fillets and bake in a preheated 425°F until just cooked.

Provençal Stuffing

This tomato-basil stuffing is nice with salmon and trout, especially stream trout.

2 tablespoons butter
½ teaspoon minced garlic
2 tablespoons chopped onion
2 tablespoons chopped celery
2 tablespoons fresh basil (or more to taste)
1 fresh firm ripe tomato (or 2 Romas), peeled, seeded, and diced
¼ cup roasted tomatoes, chopped (see "Roasted Tomatoes" on p. 206) (optional)
2 tablespoons dry white wine or vermouth
Salt and freshly ground black pepper to taste
4 tablespoons butter
1 small clove garlic minced (or to taste)
3 cups fresh bread cubes (½- to ¾-inch dice) plus fresh crumbs if needed for consistency
1 tablespoon fresh chopped parsley
Salt and freshly ground black pepper to taste
Chicken broth or water, if needed, to moisten

In a skillet set over medium heat, sauté the garlic, onion, and celery in the butter until the celery is tender-crisp. Add basil and both kinds of tomatoes and cook for a minute or so. Add dry white wine and cook until liquid is slightly reduced, about 1 minute. Season to taste with salt and pepper and scrape into a large bowl. Set aside while preparing bread cubes.

Melt the remaining butter in a large skillet set over medium heat and sauté the garlic for 30 seconds without browning. Add the bread cubes and sauté, tossing and stirring, until coated with the garlic butter and very lightly browned. Add sautéed bread to the tomato-basil mixture. Add the chopped parsley and toss gently. Taste carefully for seasoning, adding salt and pepper if necessary. If necessary, moisten stuffing with chicken stock or water. Makes about 4 cups stuffing.

Optional additions to this stuffing might include sliced mushrooms and/or diced green peppers (sauté with the garlic, onions, and celery), slices of ripe olives cooked wild rice and/or Parmesan cheese (add to tomato-basil mixture along with the sautéed bread cubes).

Morel Mushroom and Asparagus Stuffing

Here is a stuffing that captures the essence of spring when wild morels and wild asparagus tempt the forager. Farm-raised morels (plus other wild mushrooms) and seasonal asparagus can, of course, be found in many supermarkets. This is especially good with trout or salmon.

4 tablespoons butter
1 teaspoon minced garlic
½ cup minced onions
2 cups coarsely chopped morel mushrooms (or substitute other wild mushrooms or a combination of wild and white or crimini mushrooms)
Knorr® Aromat All-Purpose Seasoning or salt to taste
¼ cup dry white vermouth or dry white wine
4 cups coarse fresh bread crumbs
Light chicken stock or cream or a combination, as needed to moisten
1 cup coarsely chopped cooked asparagus
2 tablespoons chopped parsley
2 tablespoons freshly grated Parmesan cheese (optional)
Knorr® Aromat All-Purpose Seasoning and freshly ground black pepper to taste
Drops of fresh lemon juice to taste

In a skillet set over medium-low heat, sauté garlic and onions in butter until soft but not browned. Increase heat to medium and add chopped mushrooms. Season to taste with Aromat seasoning. Cook, tossing occasionally, until mushrooms are soft and any juices they give off have been reduced to dry. Add vermouth or dry white wine and reduce to 1 tablespoon. Scrape into bowl and stir in asparagus, parsley, and bread crumbs. Add enough cream to make a moist stuffing. Season to taste with additional Aromat seasoning and pepper.

Use a food processor with a metal blade to make the bread crumbs. A 1-pound loaf of French or Italian bread with crusts removed makes about 2 quarts of fresh bread crumbs.

Shrimp Stuffing

A rich buttery stuffing that is especially good with walleye.

2 tablespoons butter
2 tablespoons chopped green or red pepper or 1 tablespoon of each
2 tablespoons chopped onions
1 small clove garlic, minced
1 quart fresh white bread crumbs
5 ounces chopped cooked shrimp (or other cooked seafood, such as lobster)
2 tablespoons chopped parsley or chives
6 tablespoons melted butter
Light chicken stock or clam juice, as needed to moisten stuffing
½ teaspoon salt, or to taste
¼ teaspoon white pepper
Drops of fresh lemon juice to taste
Drops of hot pepper sauce to taste

In a skillet set over medium-low heat melt butter and sauté garlic, onions, and green peppers until onions are transparent. Scrape into a large bowl. Mix in bread crumbs, chopped cooked shrimp, and parsley or chives and combine well. Mix in melted butter and add chicken stock or clam juice to moisten stuffing as desired. Season to taste with salt, white pepper, and drops of lemon juice and hot pepper sauce to taste.

Spinach, Mushroom, and Parmesan Stuffing

This flavorful spinach stuffing is made moist with the addition of sour cream and fresh eggs. It goes especially well with salmon, lake trout, and stream trout.

4 tablespoons butter

8 ounces fresh mushrooms, sliced

¼ cup finely chopped onions

2 10-ounce packages frozen spinach, cooked according to package directions, cooled, squeezed dry, and chopped

½ cup sour cream

2 eggs, lightly beaten

½ cup herb-seasoned stuffing cubes (your favorite brand)

¼ cup freshly grated Parmesan cheese

Salt and freshly ground black pepper to taste

Roasted Tomatoes

Roasting tomatoes concentrates their flavor. Consider roasted tomatoes a fresher tasting alternative to sundried. Roasting is also an excellent way to preserve your own homegrown tomatoes since the roasted ones freeze well.

Roma tomatoes, stem end cut off and halved lengthwise

Olive oil

Salt and freshly ground black pepper

Preheat oven to 250°F. In a large bowl toss tomato halves with olive oil to coat and arrange with cut side up on a baking sheet. Sprinkle tomatoes lightly with salt and pepper.

Roast for 2 to 3 hours or until tomatoes are about ½ to ¾ dried; they should be somewhat similar to dried apricots but a little juicier. *Store in covered container in refrigerator for up to 3 days or freeze for up to 6 months.*

Note: Sundried tomatoes that have been covered with boiling water and soaked for 30 minutes, then drained and chopped or julienned may be substituted for roasted tomatoes. Since dried tomatoes are more concentrated in flavor, use slightly less or add to taste.

In a 10-inch skillet set over medium heat, melt the butter and when the foam subsides, sauté the mushrooms and the onions until soft but not browned. Scrape into a bowl and add the spinach, sour cream, beaten eggs, stuffing cubes, and Parmesan cheese. Toss to combine well and season to taste with salt and pepper. Makes about 4 to 5 cups.

Northwoods Wild Rice Stuffing

Here is a versatile stuffing made with Minnesota wild rice and seasoned with smoked bacon and studded with toasted pine nuts. This is excellent with all fish.

> 3 tablespoons butter, melted
> 3 cups cubed bread
> 3 slices bacon, diced
> ½ shallot, chopped
> ½ small onion, chopped
> 2 to 3 tablespoons chopped leeks (optional)
> ¼ cup pine nuts
> 1½ cups cooked wild rice (about ½ cup uncooked)
> Chicken broth, homemade or canned low-sodium, as needed to moisten stuffing
> Salt and freshly ground black pepper to taste

Preheat oven to 300°F. Toss bread cubes with melted butter and spread out on a sheet pan. Bake in preheated oven until lightly browned and mostly crisp, about 15 to 25 minutes or so.

Toast the pine nuts in a 350°F oven for 8 to 10 minutes until lightly browned.

Meanwhile, in a medium-sized skillet, sauté bacon until crisp. Remove from pan and reserve, leaving drippings behind. Sauté shallot, onion, and the optional leeks in the bacon drippings until the onion is transparent.

Toss the toasted bread cubes, the reserved bacon, the shallot-bacon dripping mixture, the toasted pine nuts, and the cooked wild rice together. Moisten with chicken broth as desired and season to taste with salt and pepper. Makes about 4 cups of stuffing.

Breadings

One morning some years ago as I sat sipping coffee in the kitchen of the Chippewa Inn, located on Saganaga Lake, Ontario, I observed a fisherman passing through with a can of evaporated milk in hand and a box of Ritz® crackers tucked under his arm. It was obvious he was hoping to catch enough fish for a noontime fish fry. In his hands he carried the soul of a northwoods shore lunch—the simple ingredients for breading fish. Below you will find a recipe for an all-purpose breading mix you can use to create a multitude of breadings.

Northwoods All-Purpose Breading Mix

This may be the only breading mix you will ever need. And it's not only for fish. By itself it can be used as a seasoned flour, or as a light breading for fried foods of all kinds, or as the first step of a three-step breading process. Add some cornmeal or cracker meal and you will have the breading popular with fishing guides. And if you like beer batter, simply mix it with beer and you'll have the best beer batter I have ever found.

Small Recipe:

> 1½ cups all-purpose flour
> 1 tablespoon salt
> 1½ teaspoons freshly ground black pepper
> 1½ tablespoons paprika

Combine all ingredients in a bowl and whisk together. Store in an airtight container or plastic bag in a cool dark spot until needed.

Large Recipe:

> 1 pound 4 ounces all-purpose flour
> ¼ cup salt
> 2½ tablespoons black pepper
> 6 tablespoons paprika

Combine all ingredients in a large bowl and whisk until well mixed. *May be made several months ahead and stored in an airtight container or plastic bag in a cool dark spot until needed.*

Guide's Breading

This is the breading used by fishing guides all over the north for frying fish for shore lunch.

> 1 cup Northwoods All-Purpose Breading Mix
> ⅓ cup cornmeal or cracker meal (more as desired)

Combine all ingredients in a plastic bag. To use, shake fillets in breading and deep-fry until golden brown.

For variety, use instant potato buds or granules in place of the cornmeal or cracker meal.

The Best Beer Batter

Absolutely the best.

> 1 cup Northwoods All-Purpose Breading Mix
> Beer, as needed to make a batter as thick as paint

To use, dredge fish fillets in plain flour, then dip into the batter and deep-fry until golden brown.

Beer Corn Batter

The cornmeal adds a satisfying crunch to this batter. Add a stick and you'd have Pronto Pisces—a corn fish dog. But would walleye on a stick sell at the Minnesota State Fair?

> 1 cup Northwoods All-Purpose Breading Mix
> ½ cup cornmeal
> 1 teaspoon dry mustard
> ⅛ teaspoon cayenne pepper
> Beer, as needed

Combine dry ingredients and whisk in enough beer to make a batter as thick as paint. Dredge fish in plain flour, shaking off the excess and dip into batter. Deep-fry until golden brown.

Three-Step Breading

This breading is also called Anglaise or English breading.

> 1½ cups Northwoods All-Purpose Breading Mix (or as needed)
> 2 eggs beaten with 1/2 cup water, white wine, milk, evaporated milk, cream, beer, or other liquid
> Dry or fresh bread crumbs, panko flakes (Japanese bread crumbs), crushed crackers, bread crumbs mixed with freshly grated Parmesan or Romano cheese, finely chopped pecans, cashews, or other nuts, or fresh or dried herbs.

Dredge fish in Northwoods All-Purpose Breading Mix, shaking off the excess, then dip into the egg mixture and finally into the breading mixture, using your hand to coat the fish. Bread all the fish and lay in a single layer on a platter or pan. Fish may be fried immediately or refrigerated uncovered for up to an hour or so. Refrigerating the fish for a while sets up the breading so it adheres better.

Fresh fish that have been breaded with Three-Step Breading may also be frozen with great success (see p. 10).

Ron Berg's Game-Fish Seasoning

Here is my general purpose seasoned salt for all manner of fish. Use it to season fish before searing, broiling, grilling, or baking, in stuffings and breadings, or wherever you want a boost in flavor.

½ cup kosher salt

1½ teaspoons granulated garlic

2 teaspoons lemon pepper seasoning (your favorite brand)

1½ teaspoons celery salt

1½ teaspoons onion powder

2 teaspoons Cajun seasoning (p. 212 or your favorite brand)

1 teaspoon medium-coarse freshly ground black pepper

2 tablespoons paprika

½ teaspoon cornstarch

Combine all ingredients in a small bowl and mix well. Makes about ¾ cup. *Store in an airtight container in a cool dark place.*

Kosher Salt

Chefs prefer kosher salt for a couple of reasons. First, because it is coarser than regular salt, it is easier to pick up with the fingers, the chef's favorite way to season foods. Second because it has no additives, it tastes less bitter than regular salt. Buy a box of kosher salt and compare how it tastes with your regular salt. Because kosher salt has bigger crystals that pack more loosely, less salt goes into your measuring spoon. Measure for measure, you will need to use about one-third more kosher salt than regular table salt.

Cajun Seasoning

Excellent for blackening fish or grilling.

1 tablespoon dried basil
1 tablespoon garlic powder
1 tablespoon gumbo filé (optional)
1 tablespoon dry mustard
1 tablespoon onion powder
1 tablespoon dried oregano
¼ cup paprika
¼ cup ground black pepper
1 tablespoon cayenne pepper
1 tablespoon ground white pepper
½ cup kosher salt
1 tablespoon dried thyme
½ teaspoon cornstarch

In a medium bowl, combine all ingredients and mix thoroughly. Makes about 1½ cups. *Store in an airtight container in a cool dark place.*

Ron's Creole Seasoning

Similar to Cajun. Use in Creole-style dishes.

  6 tablespoons kosher salt
  ½ cup paprika
  6 tablespoons garlic powder
  3 tablespoons onion powder
  3 tablespoons black pepper
  3 tablespoons cayenne pepper
  1 tablespoon white pepper
  3 tablespoons dried oregano
  3 tablespoons dried thyme
  ¼ teaspoon cornstarch

In a medium bowl, combine all ingredients and mix thoroughly. Makes about 2¼ cups. *Store in an airtight container in a cool dark place.*

Chapter 10

Sauces for Fish

ome say that sauces were invented in the days before reliable refrigeration to cover the taste of food that had started to spoil. Whatever the reason, the French are acknowledged to be the world's master sauciers. They have even gone so far as to arrange their sauces into families consisting of mother sauces (also called leading sauces), secondary sauces, and small sauces. Hence Fish Velouté would be classified as a mother sauce; from this is derived the secondary sauce, White Wine Sauce. From these two sauces are derived several small sauces, such as Fresh Herb, Bercy, Mushroom, and Champagne.

Also in this chapter you will find some old favorites to serve with fish, such as tartar sauce and cocktail sauce, plus other sauces sure to become new favorites. You'll also learn how to prepare the popular classics, hollandaise and beurre blanc, sauces which themselves have numerous variations.

Stocks

Besides being quick and easy to make, fish stocks are an invaluable resource to have on hand for making a vast array of soups, chowders, and flavorful sauces. Any of the following stocks may be made up to 3 days ahead and stored in a covered container in the refrigerator, or they may be frozen for up to 6 months. Make stock in the summer when the fish are plentiful and freeze it in 1- or 2-cup containers for use in the winter months. In a pinch, bottled clam juice may be substituted for fish stock in most recipes. Be sure to allow for the extra salt content of the clam juice.

White Wine Fish Stock or Fumet

Use the smaller amount of trimmings to make a stock that's perfect for a fine fish chowder or for poaching fish; use the larger amount of trimmings to make a stock suitable for rich sauces. Reserve the heads and bones from any nonoily fish you catch (avoid salmon and lake trout), discarding the skin and gills, to use for making this stock.

> 1 to 2 pounds (about 4 to 8 cups) fish frames and heads
> ½ cup finely chopped onion
> ⅔ cup dry white vermouth or dry white wine
> 3½ to 4 cups cold water to cover
> 2 teaspoons fresh lemon juice
> ½ teaspoon dried thyme, crumbled
> 6 whole black peppercorns
> 2 parsley stems

In a large saucepan, combine fish frames and heads, onion, and dry white vermouth or white wine. Bring to a boil over high heat and reduce the wine by one half. Add enough cold water to cover the bones by ½ inch. Add the remaining ingredients and bring to a simmer. Simmer slowly uncovered for thirty minutes. Strain through a very fine sieve or through washed cheesecloth. *May be made up to 3 days ahead and stored in a covered container in the refrigerator or frozen for up to 6 months.* Makes about 3 to 4 cups.

Improved Clam Juice for Stock

While clam juice itself is a fine substitute for fish stock, this recipe produces a fish stock similar to one made with white wine. Use this in any recipe that calls for fish stock.

1½ cups bottled clam juice
1 cup water
⅔ cup dry white vermouth or dry white wine
½ cup finely chopped onions
3 whole black peppercorns

Combine all ingredients in a saucepan. Bring to a simmer and cook for 30 minutes. Strain the stock. *May be made up to 3 days ahead and stored in a covered container in the refrigerator or frozen for up to 6 months.* Makes about 2 cups.

Court Bouillon

This is the classic French poaching broth for fish and seafood.

2 quarts water
½ cup white wine vinegar or lemon juice
½ cup thinly sliced onions or the green leaves of a leek
¼ cup thinly sliced celery
¼ cup thinly sliced carrots
1 tablespoon kosher salt
4 crushed black peppercorns
½ bay leaf
6 parsley stems

Combine all ingredients in a large nonreactive saucepan and bring to a boil. Reduce heat and simmer for 30 minutes. Remove from heat and cool. Strain before using. *May be made up to 3 days ahead and stored in a covered container in the refrigerator or frozen for up to 6 months.*

Classic French Sauces for Fish

Fish Velouté

In French cookery, a Velouté (vee-LOOT-tay) is nothing more than a roux (flour and butter) thickened stock. The following fish Velouté is not used as a sauce itself; rather it is used as a versatile base for preparing sauces of all kinds. For that reason the Velouté is not seasoned at all. Two of the most common sauces derived from a fish Velouté are White Wine Sauce, which lends itself to numerous variations, and an elegant Champagne Sauce (recipes below). The following procedure may be followed to make a chicken, beef, or veal Velouté simply by using the appropriate stock.

> 1½ tablespoons butter
> 1½ tablespoons flour
> 2 cups fish stock or bottled clam juice, plus more as needed (p. 216, 217)

Heat the fish stock in a saucepan until hot but not boiling. In another heavy-bottomed saucepan set over low heat, melt the butter. Whisk in the flour and cook, stirring occasionally, until the roux just starts to turn a slightly darker color, but no more. You definitely do *not* want to brown the roux. Cool the roux slightly, then whisk in the hot fish stock. Increase heat to medium high and continue whisking constantly until mixture thickens and comes to a boil. Reduce heat to low and simmer very slowly for about an hour, stirring occasionally. Add more stock as necessary if the sauce begins to get too thick. Strain through a fine strainer. *May be made up to 3 days ahead and refrigerated or may be frozen for up to 3 months.* Makes about 2 cups.

White Wine Sauce

White Wine Sauce is a classic sauce for fish. It, or any of the variations that follow, is perfect for saucing poached, broiled, baked, and roasted fish.

¼ cup dry white wine
2 cup Fish Velouté (see p. 218)
¼ cup heavy cream
1 tablespoon butter
Salt, white pepper, and drops of fresh lemon juice to taste

In a saucepan set over medium-high heat, reduce the wine by half. Add Fish Velouté and increase heat to medium. Simmer until reduced to a saucelike consistency. Slowly whisk in the cream. Remove from heat and swirl in the butter. Season to taste with salt, white pepper, and drops of lemon juice. Strain through a fine strainer. *May be made up to 3 days ahead and refrigerated covered or frozen for up to 3 months.* Makes about 2¼ cups.

Variations of Fish Velouté and White Wine Sauce

Mushroom Sauce:

Sauté 1 cup of sliced white mushrooms in a little butter with a few drops of lemon juice to help keep them white and add to 2 cups White Wine Sauce.

Fresh Herb Sauce:

Add chopped parsley, chives, and tarragon (or basil) to taste to White Wine Sauce.

Bercy Sauce:

In a skillet set over medium-high heat, combine ¼ cup dry white wine with 2 tablespoons finely chopped shallots and reduce by ⅔. Add to 2 cups Fish Velouté and simmer slowly for 10 minutes. Just before serving, add a tablespoon each of cold butter and chopped parsley and stir until butter is melted. Taste and add a few drops of fresh lemon juice if desired.

Champagne Sauce

This sauce adds élan to many fish dishes, including the elegant Walleye Stuffed with Salmon Mousseline on a Bed of Spinach with Champagne Sauce (p. 116).

> 8 ounces (1 cup) brut champagne
> 2½ tablespoons minced shallots
> 2 cups Fish Velouté
> 6 tablespoons heavy cream
> 1 tablespoon butter
> Salt, white pepper, and drops of fresh lemon juice to taste

In a saucepan set over high heat, reduce the champagne with the shallots by ⅔. Reduce heat to low and whisk in the Velouté. Simmer slowly for 10 minutes or until reduced to desired consistency. Slowly whisk in the cream. Remove from heat and swirl in the butter. Season to taste with salt, white pepper, and drops of lemon juice. Strain through a fine strainer. *May be made up to 3 days ahead and refrigerated covered or frozen for up to 3 months.* Makes about 2⅓ cups.

Sauce Mornay for Fish

Sauce Mornay is a classic French cheese sauce that has many variations. Here is a version that is eminently suitable for fish. It is excellent sauce to serve over broiled or baked fish. It is also a key ingredient in Walleye Florentine.

> 4 tablespoons butter
> 4 tablespoons flour
> Pinch cayenne pepper
> 1 cup milk
> ¼ cup heavy cream
> ½ cup White Wine Fish Stock (p. 216) or bottled clam juice
> 3 tablespoons dry white vermouth or dry white wine
> ¼ cup shredded Gruyère or Swiss cheese
> ¼ cup freshly grated Parmesan cheese
> Salt and ground white pepper to taste
> Drops of fresh lemon juice

In a saucepan set over medium-low heat, melt the butter. Make a roux by whisking in the flour and the cayenne pepper and cooking for 2 minutes without browning, stirring occasionally. Remove from heat and let cool for a minute or so. In a bowl combine the milk, cream, fish stock or clam juice, and the wine. Add all at once to the roux and whisk to incorporate. Return pan to medium heat and cook, stirring constantly, until the mixture comes to a boil and is thickened and smooth. Stir in the cheeses and remove from heat. Let sit, stirring occasionally, until cheese is melted. Season to taste with salt, white pepper, and drops of lemon juice to taste.

If the sauce becomes too thick, thin with additional milk.

Walleye Florentine

Preheat oven to 400°F. Spread a ½-inch layer or so of cooked spinach that has been coarsely chopped and seasoned with salt, pepper, and a dash of nutmeg in the bottom of a buttered, shallow-sided casserole dish. Place walleye fillets on top of the spinach in a slightly overlapping layer. Spoon the Mornay Sauce over the top of the fish to cover and sprinkle with additional grated cheeses. Bake in preheated oven for 15 to 30 minutes or until fish is barely done.

Cold Sauces

Basic Tartar Sauce

    1 cup mayonnaise
    1 finely chopped dill pickle (about 3 to 4 tablespoons)
    1 tablespoon minced onion
    1 tablespoon drained chopped capers (optional)
    1 tablespoon chopped parsley
    ½ teaspoon crumbled dried tarragon
    1 teaspoon sugar
    ¼ teaspoon salt (or to taste)
    1 teaspoon prepared mustard (the yellow ballpark kind)
    ½ teaspoon lemon juice
    1½ tablespoons finely chopped pimento-stuffed olives (optional)
    1 hard-boiled egg, finely chopped (optional)
    Freshly ground black pepper to taste

Combine all ingredients and refrigerate for at least 1 hour before serving. Makes about 1¼ cups. Keep refrigerated.

Jalapeño Tartar Sauce

    1 cup mayonnaise
    1½ tablespoons minced red onion
    2 tablespoons minced jalapeños, seeds and stem removed (more to taste)
    1½ teaspoons sugar
    1 tablespoon prepared yellow mustard (the yellow ballpark kind)
    ½ teaspoon fresh lemon juice
    ½ cup finely chopped dill pickle
    1 tablespoon chopped parsley
    ⅛ teaspoon freshly ground black pepper

Combine all ingredients. Refrigerate until needed. Makes about 2½ cups.

Chopped bottled or canned pickled jalapeños may be substituted to taste for the fresh ones.

Horseradish Tartar Sauce

1 cup mayonnaise
1 tablespoon horseradish
1½ tablespoons red onions, finely minced
6 tablespoons dill pickles, finely chopped
1 teaspoon Dijon mustard
1 teaspoon fresh lemon juice
1¼ teaspoons sugar
¼ teaspoon salt
A pinch of pepper
1 tablespoon ketchup
1 dash hot sauce
1 tablespoon chopped fresh parsley

In a medium bowl combine all ingredients; mix well. Refrigerate 1 hour before serving to combine the flavors. Store in refrigerator. Makes about 1½ cups.

Chive-Horseradish Sauce

This is excellent with smoked fish.

1 cup mayonnaise
2 tablespoons horseradish (or to taste)
Pinch of salt
2 tablespoons chopped chives or green onion tops

Combine and refrigerate until needed.

Cocktail Sauce

½ cup chili sauce

⅓ cup ketchup

2 tablespoons prepared horseradish

¼ teaspoon salt

¼ teaspoon Worcestershire sauce

1 dash hot pepper sauce (optional)

Combine all ingredients and refrigerate until needed. Makes about 1 cup.

Tomato-Basil Remoulade

This is a variation on a recipe of Bob Bennett's, chef-owner of Bennett's on the Lake in Duluth, Minnesota. This mildly piquant sauce is a superb accompaniment for fish and seafood of all kinds.

2 ripe but firm tomatoes, peeled, seeded, and cut into ¼-inch dice

2½ tablespoons finely chopped red onion

2½ tablespoons chopped fresh basil

¼ teaspoon kosher salt

Freshly ground black pepper to taste

¼ to ½ teaspoon sugar or to taste

¾ teaspoon red vinegar

1⅓ cups mayonnaise

1 tablespoon coarse-grain mustard, such as Pommery or Creole

1 to 2 shakes hot pepper sauce (more to taste)

Combine all ingredients in a large bowl and mix well. Taste and adjust seasoning, adding additional salt and sugar to taste. Refrigerate until needed. Makes about 3 cups.

Curry-Dijon Mayonnaise

This versatile sauce makes a great dipping sauce (try cold whole green beans cooked al dente), sandwich spread, and sauce for fried or broiled fish. Try it also as a topping for baked fish.

½ cup mayonnaise
1 to 2 teaspoons curry powder (or to taste)
1 to 1½ teaspoons Dijon mustard (or to taste)

Combine all ingredients and mix well. Refrigerate until needed. Makes about ½ cup.

Curry-Dijon Crusted Fish

Spread a layer of Curry-Dijon Mayonnaise on top of boneless, skinless fish fillets that have been placed skin side down on a buttered pie tin or shallow-sided sheet pan. Sprinkle dry or fresh bread crumbs over the mayonnaise and then sprinkle lightly with paprika. Bake in a preheated 375°F oven until crumbs are lightly browned and the fish is barely cooked through.

Cucumber Sauce

1 medium cucumber, peeled, seeded, and diced
1 teaspoon kosher salt
2 teaspoons Dijon mustard
½ cup mayonnaise
Salt and freshly ground black pepper to taste

Toss diced cucumbers with the salt and refrigerate for 15 minutes. Drain well and blot dry with paper towels. Combine with the remaining ingredients and refrigerate until ready to use. Makes about ¾ cup.

Desert Paint Sauces

The Southwestern flavors and pastel colors of the next four sauces gave rise to their name. Use them individually or in combination for stunning colorful presentations. (See also p.105.)

Fire-Roasted Red Pepper Remoulade

> 2 roasted red peppers, peeled, seeded, pureed, and strained
> 1⅓ cups mayonnaise
> 2 teaspoons fresh lime juice (or to taste)
> Salt and freshly ground black pepper to taste

Combine roasted red pepper puree and mayonnaise in the bowl of a food processor fitted with a metal blade. Blend together, adding fresh lime juice, salt, and pepper to taste. Put in plastic squeeze bottle to use. *May be made up to 2 weeks ahead and stored in the refrigerator.* Makes about 1⅓ cups.

Smoked Yellow Pepper Remoulade

> 2 smoked yellow peppers, peeled and seeded
>   (smoking directions on p. 175)
> 1⅓ cups mayonnaise
> Juice of ½ lime (or to taste)
> ½ canned chipotle *en adobo,* minced, plus ½ teaspoon *adobo* sauce
>   (or to taste)
> Salt and fresh ground black pepper to taste

Combine all ingredients in a food processor with a metal blade and puree. Put through a fine strainer. Refrigerate until needed. Put in plastic squeeze bottle to use. May be made up to 2 weeks ahead and stored in the refrigerator. Makes about 1⅓ cups.

Green Chile Aioli

1 cup mayonnaise
1 teaspoon minced garlic
1 poblano chile, peeled, seeded and cut into 1-inch pieces
½ peeled and seeded jalapeño (optional)
1 tablespoon fresh lime juice or to taste
Salt and freshly ground black pepper to taste

To make aioli, place mayonnaise, garlic, poblano chile, and lime juice in a food processor and process with a metal blade until pureed. Season to taste with salt and pepper. Strain through a sieve and put into a plastic squeeze bottle. Refrigerate until needed. *May be made up to 2 weeks ahead and stored in the refrigerator.* Makes about 1¼ cups.

Mexican Crema

1 cup sour cream, regular or lowfat
Drops of freshly squeezed lime juice to taste
Salt to taste
Half-and-half to thin, as needed

Combine all ingredients and whisk well. Store in plastic squeeze bottle in the refrigerator. Makes about 1 cup. *May be made up to 2 weeks ahead and stored in the refrigerator.*

Compound Butters for Fish

The following flavored butters keep well in the freezer and add delicious, rich, savory flavor to grilled, broiled, poached, or baked fish. Use plastic wrap or parchment paper to form the following compound butters into a round roll about 1-inch in diameter. For fancier presentation, the butter may be piped out into rosettes using a pastry bag and a fluted tip. Let the butter come to room temperature before serving on the fish.

Maître d'Hôtel Butter

This classic compound butter is often served with grilled or broiled steaks. Its lemony flavor complements fish perfectly as well.

> 1 stick (4 ounces) butter, softened
> 1 tablespoon chopped parsley
> 2 to 2½ tablespoons fresh lemon juice to taste
> Pinch of white pepper

Cream the butter with a mixer or a wooden spoon. Add the remaining ingredients and beat until incorporated.

Beurre d'Escargot

Literally this means "butter for snails," but it is nothing more than garlic butter with shallots and parsley. It is delicious spread over grilled or broiled fish just before serving.

> 1 stick (4 ounces) butter, softened
> 1 tablespoon finely chopped shallots
> 1 to 1½ teaspoons finely chopped garlic (more to taste)
> 2 tablespoons finely chopped parsley
> Kosher salt and freshly ground black pepper to taste

Cream butter with a mixer or wooden spoon. Beat in remaining ingredients.

Garlic-Herb Butter

Use this compound butter like the Beurre d'Escargot above, which it resembles. It makes great hot garlic bread and fresh mushrooms sautéed in Garlic-Herb Butter are highly recommended.

> 12 tablespoons butter
> 2 cloves garlic, minced
> ¼ teaspoon salt (or to taste)
> 1½ teaspoons fresh tarragon leaves, finely chopped, or ½ teaspoon dried, crumbled
> 1 tablespoon chopped parsley
> 1 teaspoon fresh lemon juice

Cream butter with a mixer or wooden spoon. Beat in remaining ingredients, adding lemon juice little by little at the end.

Bercy Butter

Bercy Butter is a delicious flavored butter of great versatility. Besides its affinity for fish, it is a wonderful topping for grilled or broiled steaks of all kinds and baked potatoes. Like the Garlic-Herb Butter above, this butter makes great garlic bread and sautéed mushrooms.

> 1 stick (4 ounces) butter, softened
> 1 tablespoon minced shallots
> 1 teaspoon minced garlic (more to taste)
> 1 tablespoon chopped parsley
> 1 teaspoon dry white vermouth or dry white wine
> ½ teaspoon lemon juice
> Salt to taste

Cream butter with a mixer or wooden spoon. Beat in remaining ingredients.

Whole-Grain Mustard Shallot Butter

This is especially good with lake trout or salmon.

> 1 stick (4 ounces) butter, softened
> 1 tablespoon whole-grain French or Creole mustard
> 1 tablespoon minced shallots
> ¼ teaspoon salt (or to taste)
> ¼ teaspoon freshly ground black pepper (or to taste)

Cream butter with a mixer or wooden spoon. Beat in remaining ingredients.

Butter Sauces for Fish

Hollandaise and beurre blanc sauces are both emulsion sauces. An emulsion is a mixture of two unmixable liquids. These sauces both contain a mixture of butter and water (which includes the water in the lemon juice or vinegar). In both sauces, the two stay mixed because the butter is added in the form of droplets to an emulsifier—egg yolks in the hollandaise, and high acidity in the beurre blanc—which holds the droplets of butter and water apart. Hollandaise sauce is an emulsion sauce made with egg yolks, butter, lemon juice, and seasonings. It is best known as the sauce for Eggs Benedict. It is a delicious sauce for salmon, lake trout, and any stream trout.

Hollandaise Sauce

Make sure all of your equipment is perfectly clean. The eggs and the temperature of a finished hollandaise are ideal for bacterial growth. For the same reason, use the sauce within 1 hour of completing.

Although experienced chefs are able to heat the yolks over direct heat, the hot water method described below is safer, though slower. As your confidence increases, you will be able to use a hotter heat source and make the sauce more quickly.

A round-bottomed stainless steel bowl is best for beating the yolks evenly. Also stainless steel is nonreactive and will not discolor or give your sauce an off flavor.

Make sure the butter is not too hot or you may scramble the yolks. Also, it is of utmost importance that the butter be added very s-l-o-w-l-y at first. Finally, remember, unless the eggs have been overcooked, a broken hollandaise is usually fixable.

> 2 egg yolks
> 2 teaspoons cold water
> ⅛ teaspoon cayenne pepper
> 2 sticks of butter, melted
> 2 to 3 teaspoons fresh lemon juice (or to taste)
> Salt to taste

Combine the egg yolks, water, and cayenne pepper in a small, very clean stainless steel bowl. Beat well with a whisk. Set the bowl containing yolks over barely simmering water and whisk constantly for 5 to 10 minutes, watching the yolks carefully. The yolks are ready when they've gotten hot and thickened a little. The yolks will be frothy and will have nearly doubled in volume. If the yolks get too hot, they will scramble. If this happens you must start over, as there is no way to fix this.

Remove bowl from the heat and whisk in the melted butter, drop by drop at first until nearly half of it has been incorporated. Then the butter may be added in a thin stream until all has been added. Be careful to add only the butter fat and not the milky liquid below. Whisk in the lemon juice. If too thick, use some of the liquid from the melted butter, which is quite salty, to thin the hollandaise. Taste and season to taste with salt. The sauce may be kept for a short period in a bowl covered with film set over tepid water or in a preheated thermos for up to an hour. Makes about ¾ cup.

Fixing a Broken Hollandaise:

Pour the broken hollandaise into a glass measuring cup or small bowl. Wash and dry the stainless steel bowl and place 1 teaspoon of Dijon mustard in the bottom. Using a spoon or small ladle, whisk in the broken sauce drop by drop until an emulsion is reestablished, then very, very slowly add the remaining broken sauce. If all this fails, throw the sauce out, chalk it up to experience, and start again from the beginning.

Variations

Chive Hollandaise Sauce:

Whisk in ½ teaspoon Dijon mustard and 2 tablespoons chopped fresh chives with the lemon juice in the recipe above.

Smoked Tomato Hollandaise:

Whisk in 1 tablespoon or more to taste of Smoked Tomato Puree (p. 172).

Ron's Beurre Blanc

Beurre blanc is sometimes referred to as a hollandaise without egg yolks. Like hollandaise, beurre blanc is an emulsion made with butter (unsalted preferred since it contains less water than salted). Instead of egg yolks, an acidic reduction is used to bind the emulsion together, usually a combination of white wine or vermouth and a vinegar, such as champagne or white wine. White wine or vermouth alone may be used to make a beurre blanc if they are acidic enough.

My basic beurre blanc contains more white wine and less vinegar than most recipes. I also add a little cream to help stabilize the sauce. To make 1 cup, double all ingredients.

> ¾ cup dry white wine (I use chablis from a box.)
> 1 tablespoon white wine or champagne vinegar
> 1½ teaspoons finely chopped shallots
> 1 tablespoon heavy cream
> ½ cup (1 stick) unsalted butter, cut into 8 pieces
> Salt and white pepper to taste

In a 10-inch nonreactive skillet, combine the white wine, vinegar, and shallots. Bring to a boil over high heat and reduce until liquid is reduced to bubbles. Add cream and reduce until thickened, about 30 seconds or so. Add butter all at once and whisk briskly so that the butter melts evenly. When all of the butter except a small piece or two have been incorporated into the sauce, quickly pour the contents of the pan through a fine sieve into a bowl. Whisk until smooth and season to taste with salt and white pepper. At this point a handheld blender or a regular blender may be used to fluff up and thicken the beurre blanc. Use immediately or store in a preheated thermos. Makes about ½ cup.

Variations

Tomato-Basil Beurre Blanc:

Just before serving, in a warm bowl mix 2 Roma tomatoes (peeled, seeded, and diced) and ¼ cup fresh basil chiffonade (cut into thin strips) into the beurre blanc (see p. 234).

Herb Beurre Blanc:

Just before serving, in a warm bowl mix 1 to 2 tablespoons (or more to taste) of tarragon, basil, chives, parsley, or dill (or use a combination) into the beurre blanc. Dill beurre blanc is especially nice with salmon.

Basil Beurre Blanc:

This has a nice green color and great basil flavor. Place 1½ cups loosely packed fresh basil leaves and ¼ cup parsley into a blender container. Pour the finished beurre blanc over the herbs and let sit for 3 minutes. Puree in blender for one minute. Strain into a bowl and use immediately or store in thermos.

Beurre Nantais

This is the butter sauce served with the French specialty from the Nantes region, *Brochet au Beurre Blanc,* which is whole poached northern pike with white butter sauce. Try this sauce with poached northern pike fillets or with any poached fish. Any of the variations here may be used with this sauce.

¼ cup White Wine Fish Stock (p. 216), clam juice, or dry white wine
¼ cup white wine vinegar
1 tablespoon finely minced shallots
2 sticks unsalted butter, cut into 24 pieces
Salt and white pepper to taste
Drops of lemon juice to taste

In a 10-inch nonreactive skillet, combine the White Wine Fish Stock, vinegar, and shallots. Bring to a boil over high heat and reduce until liquid is reduced to a couple of tablespoons. Add butter all at once and whisk briskly so that the butter melts evenly. When all of the butter except a small piece or two have been incorporated into the sauce, quickly pour the contents of the pan through a fine sieve into a bowl. Whisk until smooth and season to taste with salt and white pepper. At this point a handheld blender or a regular blender may be used to fluff up and thicken the beurre blanc. Use immediately or store in a preheated thermos. Makes about 1¼ cups.

Index

Created by Eileen Quam

Roe, 78
Romano
  buttermilk dressing, 191
  crust, 134

Saganaga Lake, 32–33, 44, 49, 77
Salad
  Northwoods greens, 85
  potato, 190–91
  spinach, 144–45
Salad dressing. *See* Dressing,
    salad; Vinaigrette
Salmon
  availability, 147
  baked, 133, 156, 160
  broiled, 71, 162–63
  cakes, 98
  canned, 14
  caramelized, 156
  cooking time, 107
  with fettuccine Alfredo,
    150–51
  grilled, 131, 149, 162–63
  mousseline, 116–17
  panfried, 150–51, 160–61
  poached, 23
  roasted, 25, 130–31
  seared, 151, 156
  smoked, 25, 168–69
Salsa, 24, 103
  chipotle, 195
  tomato-basil, 120
Salt, kosher, 211
Salting, 165
Sauce, 81, 215–36
  aioli, 60–61, 82, 227

Alfredo, 150–53
Bercy, 219
beurre blanc. *See* Beurre Blanc
butter. *See* Butter
champagne, 116–17, 133, 138,
    220
cocktail, 30, 224
compote, tomato, 102–3
concassé, tomato, 130–31
condiment, chile-soy sauce,
    88–89
confit, tomato, 136–37
cream, 118–19, 133
Creole, 140–41
cucumber, 225
dill, 112–13
egg, 75
grilling, 148–49
herb, 219
hollandaise, 122, 170, 231–33
mayonnaise, 24, 60–61, 225
Mexican crema, 227
Mornay, 220–21
mushroom, 93–95, 118–19,
    126–27, 219
parsley-mustard, 69
pesto, 108–9
relish, cucumber-tomato, 82
remoulade, 120–21, 134, 224,
    226
salsa, 24, 103, 120, 195
sour cream, 227
southwestern, 105, 226–27
tartar, 84, 222–23
Velouté, 218–19
white, 75

Ron Berg is the chef at the Gunflint Lodge north of Grand Marais, Minnesota. He taught English to junior high students for twenty-four years and worked as a fishing guide before becoming chef at the lodge in 1990. He is coauthor, with Sue Kerfoot, of *The Gunflint Lodge Cookbook: Elegant Northwoods Dining,* published by the University of Minnesota Press.